There are a lot of men's books out there, but Xan has written a different kind of book. He walks with you as you become a man and shares with you a new vision of how great it can be to be a true man of God.

—JAN MEYERS counselor; speaker;
author of *The Allure of Hope* and *Listening to Love*

Xan, in sharing his own journey, offers a real and honest assessment of the struggles young men face in trying to find meaning, purpose, and identity. This journey unmasks the imitations and then challenges the reader to move into God's adventure, which is not easy or safe but is the only way to true manhood.

—THE REV. KEN ROSS pastor,
International Anglican Church

You're holding in your hands a rough-hewn chunk of a young man's soul. Untamed reads like an adventure novel and not some lame, squeaky-clean how-to manual. This is an authentic spiritual journey of discovery and adventure, traversing the rough terrain of real life, mistakes included!

—PETER MCKECHNIE senior pastor,
Redeemer Covenant Church, Tulsa, Oklahoma

UNTAMED

becoming the man you want to be

XAN HOOD

THINK

THiNK
P.O. Box 35001
Colorado Springs, Colorado 80935

THiNK is an imprint of NavPress.
THiNK and the THiNK logo are registered trademarks of NavPress. Absence of ® in connection with marks of NavPress or other parties does not indicate an absence of registration of those marks.

ISBN 1-57683-961-3

Cover design and illustration: BURNKIT
Creative Team: Nicci Hubert, Rick Killian, Arvid Wallen, Debby Weaver, Darla Hightower, Kathy Guist

Some of the anecdotal illustrations in this book are true to life and are included with the permission of the persons involved. All other illustrations are composites of real situations, and any resemblance to people living or dead is coincidental.

Unless otherwise identified, all Scripture quotations in this publication are taken from the HOLY BIBLE: NEW INTERNATIONAL VERSION® (NIV®). Copyright © 1973, 1978, 1984 by International Bible Society. Used by permission of Zondervan Publishing House. All rights reserved. Other versions used include: THE MESSAGE (MSG). Copyright © 1993, 1994, 1995, 1996, 2000, 2001, 2002. Used by permission of NavPress Publishing Group; the Holy Bible, New Living Translation (NLT), copyright © 1996. Used by permission of Tyndale House Publishers, Inc., Wheaton, Illinois 60189. All rights reserved; and the King James Version.

Published in association with the literary agency of Alive Communications, Inc., 7680 Goddard Street, Suite 200, Colorado Springs, CO 80920 (www.alivecommunications.com).

Hood, Xan, 1978-
   Untamed : becoming the man you want to be / Xan Hood.
      p. cm.
   Includes bibliographical references.
   ISBN 1-57683-961-3
   1. Men (Christian theology) 2. Christian men--Religious life. 3. Masculinity--Religious aspects--Christianity. I. Title.
   BT703.5.H66 2006
   248.8'42--dc22

                              2006009346

Printed in the United States of America

1 2 3 4 5 6 7 8 9 10 / 10 09 08 07 06

For my new bride,
Jayne.

the wildland

I hear there's a place
With something so wild
And something so reckless
Where love is brave
And every risk taken is another way

There was nothing I could say
Just closed my eyes
And I walked through the gate
And for once in my life
I'm finding who I am

And I walk with the Lion
As a lamb into the wildland.

— JUSTIN CARLSON, SINGER AND SONGWRITER

Contents

acknowledgments

There are so many people I want to thank.

Dan Allender, you are my hero. Thank you for bringing the framework and grounding to these ideas through your words and your work. You are the father of so many ideas, and in some ways, the grandfather to mine.

To a group of scattered friends from Tennessee to Colorado: You are all good men and without you, this book would never have been. Eric. Rick. Jesse. Wade. Peter. David. Matt. Ben. Forest. Mike. Mark. Boyce. Clifton. Tim. Kyle. Ed. Thomas. Aaron. Justin. And Cory.

The Knoxville crew: Jonathan, Sherman, Jason, and Ben. I have yet to taste a group of guys with such transparency and passion for Jesus.

To the truest friend a man could ever find, Matthew McCullough. Sitting all those nights on our roof in Knoxville. Wondering, and still wondering if life with God could be what we imagined it might.

To those who took me deeper and asked me questions I would have never asked myself. Rick Kuhlman. Van Shubin. Scotty Smith. Lynn Todd. John Eldredge. And Jan Meyers and Joni Zepp with Jayne and I.

And John. Thanks for being more things to me than I have categories for. You have been a true guide in all of this. A true gift from the Father. I never would have survived without you. Thanks for saying, "Yes," even while I was punching.

The guys at 1820 Fraternity Park. In the most odd way, you taught me more about myself and life and my desires and my need for God than I could have ever found sitting around in a dorm room or on that long church pew as a kid. I hope in my story, you find hints of your own.

The finest church in town: You are not trendy, or cool, or big. You are just the International Anglican Church. And that is enough. Ken and folks, thank you.

My brother, Zac. You are a child of promise. And have more faith and courage than most grown men twice your age.

The writers who opened my heart to a real love of words, stories, and ideas. Buechner, Nouwen, Berry, Schaeffer, McLaren, Meyers (Jan), Manning, Eldredge, Willard, Miller, Allender. And the only author I read in college, Cliff.

Rick Killian. The best editor and teacher a guy could ever find. You put more work and more heart into this than ever asked, and you did it with passion and such kind guidance.

To Nicci Hubert. You brought this thing to life and believed in the idea. You are brilliant in your work and so committed. And to all the team at Navpress: Dan Rich, Darla Hightower, Andrea Christian, Melanie, Toby Lorenc, and all the others behind the scenes. Thank you for putting in the work. And taking such a risk on someone so young.

My agent. Beth Jusino. Thank you for seeing beyond the initial scribbling. You have such integrity and insight.

My family, mom and dad. You have always supported

me. And loved me. Thanks for always believing and being so proud of your two sons.

My wife. You are full of compassion, strength, tenderness, and insight. And you offered it so freely and fully as I wrote. Redemption is so sweet. And so is discovering all of it with you.

the call of the wildlands

"I will lead the blind by ways they have not known, along unfamiliar paths I will guide them."

— ISAIAH 42:16

My first encounter with God and the invitation to his great kingdom came as a ten-year-old sitting on a long church pew in an even longer building. I was convinced God was doing very well in my town — Brentwood, Tennessee. Churches like mine were scattered all over town. If the South is called the Bible Belt because of all its churches, then my town just outside of Nashville was its buckle.

I awoke Sunday mornings to my parents' announcement that it was time for church. It required getting out of bed and putting on stiff pants, itchy socks, and Sunday shoes. I really don't recall any of the sermons; I was too involved with checking off each part of the bulletin with a little pencil, drawing, and dreaming of being someplace else.

One of those places was Ohio, where I lived and played as a young boy. My friends and I would lace up our boots and set out into the forest behind my house, hiking deep into the woods that stretched for miles. We climbed jagged cliffs, skipped flat rocks in the creek beds, built damns across the river, and caught tadpoles in glass jars.

Climbing the giant trees in my wildlands created in me a thirst for risk; wading through the brook and running through the fields told me I was wild and free. This was a world to conquer and enjoy. I was an explorer, a fisherman, a bear hunter—not just some kid.

As a six-year-old, I felt alive in those woods. I wanted to be brave, strong, and free. Those wildlands were a place of freedom for all the boys who entered with me. It was a place where we could find adventures around every bend of the path.

All of this seemed to grow out of a longing for something I could not put words to at the time. I could not name the longing specifically, or tell you where it came from, or what it was about. But there it was inside of me, urging me onward. It was a calling and a cry coming from somewhere inside. It was the call that had been awakened in those woods, and it would only increase over time.

Looking back, I wonder how many hours I spent daydreaming of those times as I sat in one of those long pews. To me the woods of Ohio, my wildlands, held a freedom to be whatever I wanted to be; sitting in church was a constraint to be something I never seemed to understand.

I grew up knowing that I had to become one thing: a man. Although I didn't know what "being a man" really meant, or how I was to become one, that didn't matter—I still had to make it happen. Some things would fall in line, like the stubble on my face and the deeper voice I developed by high school, but other things, I learned, didn't happen automatically. Becoming a man would require me to do something and be someone. If I was to become a man, I was convinced I had to prove something to the world around me—especially girls—and compete for it with my friends.

Becoming a man was not an easy task, and I had no real help in figuring it out. No one I knew talked about it—no one at home, no one at church, and none of my friends. Yet it appeared we were all after it, through sports, conversations in the hallways, out on weekends, and on dates. It was something we needed to chase down and capture, and something we needed to prove to others. I knew masculinity had something to do with this internal call to prove I could answer and fulfill the questions and desires within me, desires to be strong, to be brave, to be cunning, and to do whatever I wanted; to be tough, confident, good with ladies and at sports, and be a success with anything my hands were to touch. It was a desire to be something—something that seemed to sum up what "being a man" meant.

I remember my sophomore year of high school when I got a phone call from my friend Scott. It was a short call. He and the guys were getting together to head over to Piercy Priest

Lake to go swimming and jump off the lake's surrounding limestone cliffs.

In many ways, it was a simple call to hang out. But Scott's call would be much more. It became a call to prove myself. I remember looking over the cliff's edge and into the murky, dark water of the lake below with my friends along the shoreline, waiting on me to jump. I still can recall the fear inside me, mixed with the need to be seen as brave, strong, and fearless. I had only one choice: jump. So I did.

Fulfilling this call and desire within me came again as I cranked over the engine for my first solo drive in my first car as a sixteen-year-old. Along with adventure, there came a sense of freedom and independence that the state of Tennessee and my parents had granted me. At sixteen, I had been entrusted with a powerful machine that could kill people, even myself. I was so excited and yet afraid of what I could do—the damage I might cause with this vehicle in my control. Somehow, though, that is what made it so incredible. I was in control of something dangerous, without anyone else looking over my shoulder and telling me what to do or how to do it. Just sitting in my car thrilled me. I recall spending many evenings in the front seat in the driveway, listening to Pearl Jam and dreaming of the dates, the adventures, and the road trips it would soon take me on.

I also remember Deanna—the most beautiful girl in my freshman high school class. She was the girl I wanted to date, but she was not an easy one to catch. She had the eye of every guy in school. She was also elusive, never one to be tied down to a boyfriend. It was not going to be easy, but something in me didn't want it to be easy. I wanted a challenge and a fight. There was something in Deanna and in her beauty that I needed. Something she did for the one guy who could walk down the hall with her, in his arms.

I soon discovered, however, that girls also had expectations about the guy they wanted to date. They wanted a guy with confidence, strength, and charisma—a guy who had a measure of success. From the first time I laid eyes on Deanna, I began to question if I really had what it took to be worthy of such a beautiful woman.

A common thread began to form through all these experiences. The question was, "Am I man enough?" It was a question I would ask myself a lot in the coming years.

———

These desires in me to prove myself—and the many times I failed—brought more questions. Questions that the world around me did not seem too concerned about helping me explore or answer. It seemed it was more concerned with keeping me safe *and* controlled. As a boy, my life involved seat belts, safety bars, plastic electrical inserts, child-safe pill bottles, and as I grew, warning labels and age restrictions on anything from video games to cigarettes. It always seemed that what I really wanted was just a little bit too dangerous. These desires in me needed to be restrained and controlled, not fulfilled. It wasn't long before I felt that whatever I really wanted would probably never be allowed within my reach.

I was told this was for my good, but as I grew, it felt more like arbitrary rules and restrictions, protective measures keeping me from whatever this thing inside was calling out to find.

When it came to church, religion, and God, it seemed to be the same thing. God felt like the ultimate "Safety Man." If the culture had protected me with warning labels and precautions, and the school had kept me from talking out of turn in class, it felt like the church was trying to put plastic inflatable Floaties on my heart. Although I had all these desires inside, I was taught to follow the rules, behave, and always "be careful!" Sunday school was "wholesome," youth group activities would always be "well-chaperoned," and even the Christian radio station's motto was "Safe for the whole family."

Every once in a while I did hear ideas of what it meant to be a Christian man. I heard words like *integrity, purity, character,* and *good decision-making*. But it seemed that those words, spoken by the many Christians I grew up around, only addressed what I shouldn't do. *Don't do what everyone else was doing; don't hang out at parties where temptation was too strong; don't say or watch certain things; don't this, don't that, and don't the other.* But I didn't want to be safe, nice, moral, and withheld. I wanted to live fearlessly. I wanted to be untamed. But according to the church people, the answers to my questions could be boiled down to one simple word: *Jesus*. To be wild and run through the woods? Well, that was really about my underlying desire for Jesus. And to want a hot girl hanging on my arm? That too was about Jesus. And to want to find a group of guys with whom I could explore and be wild, and jump off cliffs, and share a deep friendship? That was also all *Jesus*. I wanted to be seen as a success—well, that too was just because I needed more Jesus.

Jesus. Jesus. Jesus.

I got sick of hearing about him in pews, events, and school functions and assemblies at my Christian high school. I was told again and again he was the answer to all my questions. Everything was always to be handed over to Jesus—my desires, my life, the hunger for more. I listened to these people for a while, but it didn't seem right. Jesus sounded like the great

Hamburglar—stealing my desires, handing me a Bible verse or some prayers to recite, and giving me a list of some things to work on and a bunch of things not to do. Just sit and be a good boy and make sure my hands were clean before I ate.

The idea that God had anything to do with these desires and questions inside of me about being a man seemed a joke. Those were the things that if I got close to him, and started really praying for him to come in my life, those would be the first things he would snatch right out of my heart.

By my senior year of high school, I felt like a gerbil trapped in a cage and given a wheel to run out my adventures and dreams on. And that wheel was Jesus. All these desires and yearnings and things I wanted to do and become were to be confined to that wheel. I wanted to be independent and strong and desirable, but instead, I was to let this wheel called "Jesus" spin me and make me happy and give me peace and joy, and then I wouldn't need anything else to be content for the rest of my days.

The cage was to keep me from danger and all kinds of places that could tempt me with evil. I was to give my longings to Jesus. But he seemed not to care about my desires or want to hear my questions. And he wasn't exactly the model of what I was trying to become—he was the guy sitting with little kids on his lap patting them on the head with a few Bo Peeps by their side.

I remember feeling horrible for thinking all of this and so ashamed at not wanting to be like Jesus. But I kept wondering if there was more than God—things better than God. More fun and adventurous than God. I thought maybe God was holding out on me and life was a test to see if I would resist them or not. I imagined there were better things out there.

So for years I stayed in my cage. I was a good boy. I listened. Behaved. Trusted. And was nice and tame. I did Christian things, and I was a "Christian example" for many. But that was all on the outside. As I sat inside that cage, even with the Jesus wheel, something was calling me from outside. I was still looking out from the cage—and into the world. It was that desire and the longings that had begun in me as a child sitting in that pew. It had only grown stronger by high school. And as I approached graduation, I was finally ready to go out and find it.

So one day I did what every gerbil spends his life attempting—I escaped. I had my chance as I moved away and went to college. I'd had enough. Enough rules. Enough things I shouldn't be doing. Enough running on the wheel. Enough "safe" Christian things. One day, when no one seemed to be paying attention, I popped the lid, jumped out of the cage, and ran as far as I could from God and the Jesus wheel and all the rules. I went out and into the world with the desires of my heart for freedom and to find answers to my questions.

Honestly, I was not looking for sin or for evil, or even rebellion. I wanted just the opposite. I wanted life. Freedom. To find myself. And to find the answer to the ache in my heart for more. And to find what being a man really meant.

And so I went. Out of the cage to explore and fulfill my longings for beauty, brotherhood, success, and strength that Jesus never seemed to answer. Like the boy in the woods, I set off to answer this call in my heart, taking my desires and questions with me.

These are my adventures.

searching for life

I denied myself nothing my eyes desired;
I refused my heart no pleasure.

ECCLESIASTES 2:10

When I walked on campus at the University of Tennessee, I stepped right into the fraternity house. It was a place flowing with testosterone and promise—with guys who had found something. It was a place alive in masculinity. A place that seemed full of exactly what my heart had been searching for—life, beauty, brotherhood, and success.

The pictures and trophies on the walls told the story of the life these guys shared together. And their parties proved they had beautiful women and were tough, wild, free, and everything I had always wanted to be. They *had* the life I *wanted* to enter and explore—the life I had seen hints of as a boy—and they were not holding anything back.

So after a few beers, with the brothers cheering me on, I

signed a pledge card and joined the fraternity. I was convinced
this was it—the answer to all my heart's questions. With no
parents, no rules, and no one to tell me what to do or not to do,
I was free finally to explore and be the man I had always wanted
to be with these guys in the frat as my guides. No teachers.
No parents. No youth leaders checking up on me or making
me feel guilty. Just me and a wide, exciting, sensual world to
explore—a world filled with desire.

I stepped right into this life, and lived and breathed fraternity. I drank beer like it was water and smoked cigarettes like
I was a chimney. I spent many nights on the Knoxville strip
making my rounds at the bars with a fake ID and my band of
brothers. I was so good at partying, my fraternity elected me
as party chairman for my pledge class. I set up the bands and
called the sorority girls. Studying and even attending class came
in second to drinking beer with all my new brothers, meeting
beautiful sorority girls, and picking a few fights with other frats.
From taking girls home late at night to being carried back to
my dorm room drunk, I lived "the life." I walked into bars where
I was recognized and respected, and into classes where I knew
faces all around me. For the first time, my head was held high.
I was doing things, living things, and beings things. And I felt
like a man. I had reinvented myself. I had become a new and
improved Xan.

There's one particular party I'll never forget. I was a freshman
and had spent nearly a year with the fraternity. The party was
electric and buzzing. The place was packed with people going
in and out of rooms where beer flowed and music screamed

through the hallways and echoed down the stairs, throughout
the house, and into the courtyard where more beer was flowing. The buzz was multiplied because we had only invited *the
species: femalia*. No one else was allowed at the house except
the hundred or so members, and any girls around campus who
might want to show.

I remember stepping outside the house that night as the
evening progressed. I walked into our brick courtyard with my
friend Travis to get some air and enjoy the view. Girls were
strung like twinkle lights wrapped around the frat house. Some
were sitting on the steps, others standing together, and a few
dancing. Travis and I looked at each other wearing big smiles,
aware of the excitement and promise of our surroundings. With
our arms draped over each other's shoulders, we laughed. This
was exactly the life we had both hoped to find in college. It was
a life of desire fulfilled.

I was convinced this was life outside the cage. Life unfil-
tered. I had freedom and choices. Finally released to be what I
wanted, when I wanted, I was unleashed. It felt like I was finally
being true to myself by the choices I made—not tainted by
other people's "dos and don'ts."

I didn't let anything religious hold me back. If I wanted to
smoke something, I did; if I wanted to drink something, I went
after it; and if I saw a girl, I went after her, especially after having
some alcohol. I laughed at all those religious people who tried
to spoon-feed me their answers. Despite their attempts to keep
me from it, I had found real life.

This had to be the *real* life my Sunday school teachers and
youth ministers had been scared I might find. They had been
afraid I would find something like this and run after it, leaving everything else behind. As I sat on those frat-house steps I

thought, *How right they were.*

I felt powerful. I felt important. I was taller, bigger, and even walked with a strut.

———

But what I remember most about that party was what happened later in the night. I zigzagged my way through the freshman courtyard at 2 a.m. heading for my bed. As I walked into my dorm room, still buzzing from the beer, everything quickly changed. This room was dark. Silent. Empty. Although only ten minutes before I had been filled with energy and excitement, that "life" was gone. It was just me in that room. With the solitude came a flash of clarity.

As I sat in my room in silence, my desires and longings crept back in. They were still there—stronger than ever and still unmet. I had spent a year trying to fulfill them, but whatever satisfaction I had found in the moment, at the party, or with a girl didn't settle in or last.

I remember stumbling to the mirror, staring deeply into the glass at the person I had become. It was a bottomless stare that pierced right into my soul. I was a complete mess. What hid behind this image that stared back at me? Who was I? What had I become? And why, despite all my accomplishments and this "new me" that people seemed to like, did I still feel so hollow inside?

I was scared because I had no idea where to turn or who to follow. In the cage, I had attempted to follow God and be the nice boy, and now I had tried my own way to find a true and satisfying life—and it seemed neither worked.

A fear crept into my heart—a deep, dark, unnerving fear.

I had no idea who I was, and I knew no one around me who could help. On one hand, I knew I could find religious people to tell me the answer was to find Jesus, but on the other hand, I could also turn to the frat guy handing me a beer explaining this was the life I wanted. Neither seemed able to answer the deep ache and desires of my heart.

For months, I lived with this feeling. I didn't stop partying and drinking; I still knew something wasn't right, so I just used the beer to numb me from it. But many times and at many parties I found myself looking into mirrors of many bathrooms and wondering who it was staring back.

———

It was during this time when a man named Hank spoke at our Monday fraternity meeting. He was a campus minister and happened to be a frat man back in the day. We were not used to Christian speakers coming in, and everyone seemed to fidget in their seats. I think we were afraid of a preacher telling us about all the rules we weren't following and the sins we were committing. Hank didn't go there, though. He told some crazy stories about his days back in the fraternity, and then he started talking about Adam and Eve in the garden.

"God created man in the most unique of places. He set him in the place of life and gave him all the things he could ever need or desire. It was a place of adventure and beauty." Hank went on to explain Satan's temptation and emphasized what happened to Adam and Eve after they sinned.

He also explained that, "Before they had rebelled from God, they were naked and without shame. Loving. Laughing. Playing. But immediately after their sin, they felt shame and guilt for what they had done. They had disobeyed God and were now aware of their nakedness." He said, "Because of it, they sewed fig leaves together to cover themselves and their insecurities, and then they went and hid in the bushes, embarrassed because of what they had done." Hank explained how God called to them, and they didn't answer, and then when God finally found them, he asked Adam why they had been hiding. Hank paused, and then pulled out his Bible and read Adam's response word for word: "*I was afraid because I was naked; so I hid.*"[1]

He stopped and let us feel the weight of that statement. He stared around the room. Finally, he spoke again, "When you meet most men, what you meet is a fig leaf, a disguise, a man who is hiding. A guy pretending to be someone to be worthy of respect, love, and attention from others. A poser, a phony—a guy just like Adam." He stopped again, and looking around the room at all of us, he said, "I imagine most of the guys in here are doing it as well."

I felt a lump in my throat as we sat in an unnervingly long and awkward silence.

I knew exactly what he was talking about. I knew it so well. The scene in that mirror was haunting me.

Eventually Hank finished his talk and left. Then we continued our meeting to discuss other frat business, but I really didn't hear any of it. Hank's words stuck in my head—and my heart. He was right. I had been hiding. I was a poser.

I looked around the room as the meeting continued. I noticed how much we all looked alike, talked alike, and dressed alike. When we had joined the fraternity as new pledges, we wore different types of clothes, talked differently, and had different haircuts—but now everyone in the house seemed the same. We had the same types of backpacks, shoes, and pants. The same taste in beer and same taste in music. As I walked around campus those next few weeks, I noticed it more. I saw it in athletes, sorority girls, band members, math majors, you name it—it was everywhere. We were all doing it. All of us appeared to be hiding behind a look of confidence, covering up something inside we didn't want anyone else in the world to see.

———

If I were to really look back at my own fig leaf, I think my hiding began when I was very young. With my desires came feelings of shame and guilt and fear that I was completely inadequate and that I didn't measure up. I was embarrassed to admit who I was and—even more—who I was not. In order to get attention, to find friends, and to be a part, I felt like I had to be like the people in whatever group I was in at the time. There wasn't much room for being an individual. Because I wanted people to like me, I did what I thought would get that kind of attention and respect, even if it wasn't the real me. Because I was always fitting in, I didn't even know the real me. It seemed everyone else was becoming someone while I wasn't smart enough. Not big enough. Not good looking enough. Not talented enough. Not spiritual enough. Not cool enough.

I think it hit me around my junior year of high school that I was lacking what others had and I needed an upgrade. A new image. A new me. The answer came in the form of a red Jeep.

In high school, my car meant everything. It is what people saw, connected to me, and how they might remember and judge me. I thought it could take me to heights, or bring me success—it seemed the size of my tires, and the size of my lift, reflected the size of my mojo.

Buying a 4x4 Jeep Wrangler required crossing the toughest obstacle I had ever known: my mom's approval. It was a hard sell. My mom was scared to death of Jeeps. She saw them as death mobiles and was constantly cutting out articles of teenagers dying in Jeep or convertible accidents. She was convinced I would roll it into a ditch, twirl fifteen times in the air, and then die. So instead of confronting this, I went through my father and was somehow able to convince him; then he convinced Mom. It was a miracle. So, before she could change her mind, we found a used '91 red Wrangler in the paper and bought it that same day.

When it finally sat in our driveway, I just stood and stared at it. I sat in it. I ate in it. I washed it ten times a month, looked at it from every possible angle. I did homework in it. If it had had a diaper, I would have changed it. It was my baby. And my hope—my hope for a new me.

I think that Jeep began in much the same way I did. It had potential. When I first got the Jeep, it looked a bit girly, and smelled that way too, because we had bought it from a girl. So my first job was to scrape the flower stickers from the window, and remove the yellow pinstripes. For it to work and do what I needed it to do for me, it would require a little something out of *Pimp My Ride*. It needed to be muscled over. Beefed up. It needed to be rough, tough, and ooze with attitude. It needed to be able to step into a man's world and compete. In order to be noticed, it needed *cajones*.

I used some cash from my lawn-mowing business to fund my renovations. I worked on the car after school, in the evenings, and most of the day on weekends. It was a complete makeover.

I bolted on chrome Nerf bars, installed a new sound system, and with more money, came a suspension lift. Then wider steel rims and larger mud tires, off-road stickers, Baja lights, and a Warn winch mounted over the front bumper.

It was a beauty to behold. It grunted. When I drove down the street, people looked—young and old, guys and girls. I remember meeting people on weekends and them saying, "Oh, I know you! You're the guy with that red Jeep." Yup, that was me. I had finally been seen. My plan had worked. And so it was only natural, considering the great success of my Jeep, that I would turn to my own life and bolt on a few things there as well.

By high school, as I mentioned, you were supposed to be and look the part of a man. Even if I didn't know what it was, which I really didn't, that didn't matter. I was still supposed to be a man. I looked around for a model of what I might be. From home to school, to movies, television, magazines, and church, there were as many versions of masculinity as there were men to display them.

Was I to be strong, or soft and emotional? Should I be a ladies' man, or a man unwilling to compromise my integrity and convictions? Should I drink beer with the boys on Friday night, or head down to the church youth group lock-in? Was I going to be sensitive and poetic or tough? The life of the party or quiet and reserved? Athletic or musical? The girl's best friend or the mystery she couldn't pin down? Was I to be super spiritual? Make a lot of money? Have sex? Memorize Scripture? Be athletic? Strive for success at all costs? Stand for values? Be the wild and crazy guy? The comic? Have a girlfriend? Have three girlfriends? Stand for morals? Get a job and work hard? Be a leader? Study more? Join the Honor Society? Exactly what was I supposed to be?

I wanted to be something unique—I knew that much—someone people would notice. I wanted to stand out the way my chrome Nerf bars, Warn winch, and Mickey Thompson off-road tires did.

By high school, most people just fit a mold. They played the role they were told to by others. If a guy was good-looking and not afraid of talking to a girl, then he was the assumed ladies' man and a "stud." The smart kids were just supposed to work hard, keep their noses down, not mix with the athletes, and eventually find a career that would make them enough money so they could laugh at the dumb jocks. Being musically gifted meant you were the performer—the "music man." Sing in talent competitions, melt girls' hearts, get your name out, and maybe wear alternative clothes to match your image. Athletic? Well, then be the hero on the field and date cheerleaders. Workout, act tough, don't show emotion. And if you were overweight or unpopular? Then learn to be funny. Become the class clown. Even make fun of yourself if it was required.

Most people went with what worked easiest for them—what other people told them to be and what got them some attention. But once they had become something and were known for it, it was not over. No, that was when it became even harder—they had to live up to that image. If they were funny, they had to be funny—*all the time*. They had to keep their title and play the part everyone expected—expectations intensified, along with the pressure.

In this system, you no longer had gifts and talents; *they had you*. They defined your reputation, no matter who you really were. How you talked, laughed, and who you hung out with couldn't change—you had to fit the label: Ryan the track star, Chris the band guy, John the drunk, Matt the quarterback, Brian the brainiac, Jimmy the Jesus freak, or Jason the druggie.

Who was I to be?

This was hard. I didn't fit neatly into one category as easy as most. Nor could I choose a label I wanted more than the rest. They all had advantages. And so, through years of my life in high school and college, I tried all of them, depending on which better fit the group around me at the time. If I was around a parent, I was polite, sincere, and a good boy. At parties in college, I was loud, obnoxious, and a crudely funny jerk. At school I played the student: respectful, attentive, and polite. With friends, I was mocking and irreverent. At church, I was reserved, silent, and compliant.

Girls, however, got a custom-tailored me.

Carrie wanted a strong guy, so I worked out. Julie was looking for a bad boy, so I became James Dean. Lana wanted a romantic, so I became sensitive and thoughtful. Each new girl got a newly redesigned Xan. I played all the parts pretty well—enough to get dates at least. All an attractive girl had to do was ask, imply, or suggest; and then, like a dog fetching a stick, I put on the appropriate costume and chased down whatever it was she seemed to want.

By my sophomore year at UT, I had become an expert at the mask-wearing game I started in high school. I guess this is why people liked me, but unfortunately, it's also why I had found that guy in the mirror so disturbing. I did not know him. I was nothing more than a guy hiding behind a fig leaf.

Not too long after Hank came to the frat house, some-thing else happened to me in a lecture hall. A few friends and I had sat alone in the back, minding our own business, when a guy entered from one of the side doors. He had a limp, not a strut like I had developed. He appeared to have some kind of disability in his legs, probably from birth. He was pushing hard, slowly moving each leg to make it to a seat. It wasn't long before the whole place was looking through the corner of their eye, without giving "the stare."

As I watched him take each step, I remember thinking about how different his life must be, what the disability had kept him from experiencing — from sports, driving a car, going on dates, jumping off cliffs into a lake. I felt his pain and sadness. I wanted to help him and do something to lift his spirits, but I just watched as he kept moving one foot in front of the other, slowly moving his way to the back. He was coming closer, and then took a seat next to me. I was keyed up. I could talk to him, introduce myself. Maybe I could extend him kindness, be his friend. I figured a guy like me could make him feel important, help him out. I imagined myself a big brother or something.

So after the lecture, I introduced myself. He was a rather friendly guy. Ryan was his name. I discovered he had grown up not far from my hometown. We talked about life and school. As my curiosity finally got the better of me, I asked about his legs. "What happened?"

He told me that he had been born with a physical defect. He was quick to acknowledge all the challenges because of it. He could not play sports or run in the halls as other boys did. He almost choked up talking about it. But he said, "I was deter-mined to beat it and not let it affect my life." He had decided as a young boy to work hard and push himself, to overcome it with his will. He said, "For years, I was so angry at God. I had so many questions. I was screaming mad for him making me this way. Why would he create me with these legs? How could he let others pick on me?"

What he said next leveled me. "For years I was so bitter and angry and distant from God for making me have this limp. Everyone seeing me as being *crippled and broken*. But one day as I was yelling and screaming, God spoke to me. He said it wasn't my legs that were handicapped or broken, it was something on the inside—my heart."

We talked a few minutes more. Then he left. I walked away weighing his words. As I drove off, what he had said kept playing over and over inside of me. I did everything Ryan couldn't: sports, driving, girls, roughhousing with friends, being part of a fraternity, and even strutting. As I kept hearing that conversation play over and over in my head, I thought back to the mirror, and all those days of being someone I was not.

Tears came—but not for Ryan.

I thought about my Jeep. With the thousands of dollars spent and the almost two years working so hard on it, I had never touched anything under the hood. I had done nothing to improve the performance of the engine or enhance its components. I spent my money on what you could see on the outside, not underneath or inside. I had bought Baja lights and spent $600 on the winch, but neither worked. I never bothered to wire them. That hadn't been the point of buying them. They were to look good and to get attention, not to actually function correctly.

It was the same with me. I had spent my life putting on personalities. I had hidden behind fig leaves and masks trying to get people to like me and earn their approval. I had bolted on things, and put on a face to cover up the inside — the thing I feared the most in my life. I had never opened the hood and looked at the engine — the inside of my life, my heart — to discover what was really there. I was too afraid of what I might find — something damaged, something, as Ryan said, "broken."

Again, I realized that my life was not a life. My world was centered around pretending to be this person — the image in the mirror, the mask — trying to get people to like me by saying, doing, dressing, and being who I thought everyone else around me would like. I was afraid to share the real me. Afraid and ashamed of what people might think or say or do. The real "me" hid behind roles and personalities and masks, from my chrome to my strut. I think I was afraid, because if I had peeled back all those layers, would anything be there?

There was a gaping hole within me. I hadn't allowed myself to feel it until then, hadn't dealt with whatever it was or what I needed. I had been avoiding it. But the hole began to affect my life so much I couldn't avoid it anymore. It affected my relationships, my thoughts, my behaviors. Although I didn't know what to do, I knew this wasn't working.

deception

We look for light, but all is darkness;
for brightness, but we walk in deep shadows.
Like the blind we grope along the wall,
feeling our way like men without eyes.

ISAIAH 59:9-10

After my sophomore year of college, I drove home to Nashville for the summer. I was back home to work, play, and hang around my old friends. It was a much-needed break from my party life and the struggles I was having in college.

The real bonus, though, came in the form of my parents' new projection television, stereo, and a satellite dish with around 2,347 channels. I felt like I was in TV heaven—from the surround-sound Dolby digital receiver and DVD, to a refrigerator stocked full of food for my taking, to the new leather couch that felt like a giant pillow. My problems seemed to disappear as I camped out in front of that television. Some nights I just slept there—too lazy and comfortable to get up to go to bed. For hours that summer, after coming home at night from a friend's house, I would feast on all the music, sports, history, movie, and specialty channels.

Laying there about 1:00 a.m. one night in the second half of the summer, something shifted. As I listened to the TV hosts, the celebrities, the sports anchors, and the commercials, something occurred to me: No matter which channel I was watching, I kept hearing the same thing. I flipped to other channels, only to find someone else saying it too. Again and again. Everyone was trying to sell me something: their version of success and happiness through their product, by living their lifestyle, or by prescribing to their philosophies or politics. I kept watching their answers: the commercials that promised to get me buff and give me the perfect body from their workout machine, hook me up with the sexiest girls alive if I called their hotline, or make me a real man if I bought their off-road truck. Then the next commercial featured an average-looking dude holding a beer while dancing with three hot chicks at once. Show after show, commercial after commercial. Each was trying to sell me their answers for how to have a good and happy life, a way to be clear of all my problems and insecurities, all of them offering me the solutions and the answers for how I could almost instantly start living "the good life."

The higher the channels, the more obvious it became. The infomercials and shopping network channels were just flat out saying it: "This is exactly what you need to be happy." I started clicking with a different purpose. I hoped someone had something true and real to say, something that made some sense or brought a little clarity without my having to buy anything. Finally, after pausing to watch a few religious people in purple hair preaching from gold thrones and telling me if I sent them money I would get my needs met, I realized there was nothing left. I had surfed all 2,347 channels and found nothing real, nothing substantial, and nothing that could really fulfill me, even though they all said they had exactly what I needed.

I realized that something was wrong and broken. Not just in me, but in the world, and in other people. It was as if these advertisers and the shows were using this pain and ache we all felt inside to make money. Promising us a simple fix or a quick answer. As if what Hank said was right, we were all hiding, and insecure, and afraid. And they were selling the Band-Aids, fig leafs, and empty promises to go on the gaping wounds of the human soul. I think God was in that room that night, and he was cracking open my eyes to see that I needed something that no diet, beer, workout machine, car, or get-rich-quick scheme could satisfy. They couldn't take away the insecurities, the fears, the pain, and the brokenness we all face.

Maybe I was making too much of this—it was just television after all—but all I know is, the void in me grew deeper that night. I felt alone again. The whole world seemed full of liars telling lies I had spent most of my life listening to and believing. I remember turning off the television that night—thinking for the first time in my life of twenty years—how it all seemed so meaningless and so fake. No one was being honest or dealing with the real issues about how broken and hurting and messed up peoples lives are. Not even the religious preachers on television.

That night, I felt empty again, and cried out again, but this time instead of crying out to myself in the mirror, I cried out to God—*the* God who up to that point seemed as dark as the room I sat in. But I was desperate. And to be honest, I had run out of options. It seemed there was no place else to look, no place or no person who was willing to be honest and willing to help fix the broken things inside of me. He was my last resort. And I was that desperate.

———

Though I'd prayed, nothing much changed after that night. No miracle happened, other than what felt like a deep and sincere prayer. I still had just as many questions, if not more now that I had opened up a little to God.

Then one night back at college after summer break, I ran into a friend named Kyle. We had a few classes together and saw each other occasionally walking around campus. I ran into him at a Buddy's Bar-B-Q. I was alone, eating a sandwich and drinking some sweet tea as I studied for a test. He asked me how I was doing, and I think being so alone, and so willing, I was just honest about how I was doing. Soon, we got on the subject of the world we live in. The more I talked, the more he seemed to understand. He said he'd actually dealt with some of these same things himself—about how our lives were mostly about faking it, and about how he too had grown up thinking God was mostly about rules.

As he said more, I felt both surprised and relieved that he'd had some of the same thoughts, questions, and feelings that I had. I wasn't alone. It was a relief to find someone who had the same feelings, because up to that point I felt alone. All of those empty times happened on my own. And now, I could talk with someone else about them.

Near the end of our conversation, he gave me a CD. "You'll like it," he said. He told me it was a speaker he had heard at a conference. "This guy," he explained, "knows what's wrong with the world." Although I didn't see it at the time, it was God again, calling to me.

As I got in my car, I put in the CD and sat there in the parking lot listening. I was captivated. All this time I had felt isolated and afraid to tell anyone about what I was struggling with, and suddenly here was someone talking about it and putting words to it for me.

The man spoke about all of our desires in life — the things in each of us that we want and long for and can't figure out how to satisfy — things like beauty, adventure, freedom, and true friends to fight it with. He explained that most of us have lives that never actually fulfill the aching and calling out that's inside of us. He said that we go around finding versions of the things we want, satisfying our hearts with only a small piece of the thing we are really after.

To explain this further, he played a clip from *The Matrix*. He said it was a picture of our life on planet earth. The scene happens near the beginning of the movie when Neo walks up a staircase and into an old building as the rain pours down on him. He's responding to a call from Morpheus, who tells Neo he has the answers to his questions. Neo wants to hear more. He opens the door to see Morpheus calmly waiting for him in a chair. Neo walks into the room, bewildered, and sits down in the chair facing Morpheus.

The dialogue begins:

Morpheus: Let me tell you why you're here. What you know you can't explain, but you feel it. You've felt it your entire life, that there's something wrong with the world. You don't know what it is, but it's there, like a splinter in your mind, driving you mad. It is this feeling that brought you to me. Do you know what I am talking about?

Neo: The matrix?

Morpheus: Do you want to know what it is? The matrix is everywhere. It is all around us, even now in this very room. You can see it when you look out your window or when you turn on your television. You can feel it when you go to work, when you go to church, when you pay your taxes. It is the world that has been pulled over your eyes to blind you from the truth.

Neo: What truth?

Morpheus: That you are a slave, Neo. Like everyone else you were born into bondage, born into a prison that you cannot smell or taste or touch. A prison for your mind.[1]

After the clip played, the speaker said, "Does that sound familiar?" He proposed the idea, "What if our life was similar to this? What if we were born into a prison called 'the world'? What if we were born into a fallen world where things are not as they seem?" He went into more details and then explained, "We are all searching, exploring, and looking for answers in all sorts of places, because we are all lost and blind to our true desire. We live in a matrix, a world that has been pulled over our eyes to blind us from the truth — a truth that we cannot see or taste or touch."

In that moment, he put words to the things I had been feeling for years. I would have never thought about things this way, but after my experience with the mirror, the night of channel surfing, and Hank's talk, it seemed this man was onto something. God was speaking to me again. I don't know if this was a direct response to my prayer, but it was close. And it brought more clarity. I thought about the world I had grown up in, the world I knew in college, the cage and the Jesus wheel, and the world I entered at the University of Tennessee. It was like this man had lived through exactly the same struggles I had, but there was a confidence, and hope in his voice, as if he was now on the other side of those struggles, or at least had experienced some sense of a new life with God.

His talk shifted something inside me. A hope rose in me. It sounded good and right—up until the point he started talking about darkness and evil as being responsible for all of this, and how it was all a plot of the devil to snare us and to lead us into blindness at every turn in our life.

I wanted to believe this guy—I did—and he had me for a while, but he lost me the minute he said, "Satan." It's just that I still wasn't about to accept that there was really some evil, supernatural "mastermind" behind my problems, who was somehow leading the whole world astray and blinding *me*. That seemed way too spooky and super-religious for me.

As a little boy, I always heard rumors of bad things bad people did, and I always heard it linked with darkness and evil. I was scared of monsters under the bed, of the weird noises in the dark, the cold basement, and anything that turned black with nightfall. I hated being caught in it alone. Darkness transformed things. It brought out the bad people and green monsters. As a kid, I did my best to avoid it.

By high school, the monsters under the bed and my fear of the basement were gone, but religious people had told me of another creation that sounded much the same: the Devil. He was the horned, red-suited creature working day and night casting people into the fiery pit of darkness. Although it was freaky, I was not all that convinced. For one, the people who talked about him like this seemed a little out of touch with reality in the first place—shaking, almost foaming at the mouth, and looking devilish themselves as they spoke of him. The whole idea of this supernatural evil seemed a bit hokey, superstitious, or at least super-spiritual, if not just plain crazy. And second, I always saw Satan as the next in a long lineup of characters—from Mickey Mouse, the Tooth Fairy, the Easter Bunny, to Santa Claus—who I would soon discover was either a guy in a costume or a make-believe story church people told me because I was a gullible kid.

"The Devil" seemed just another in a long line of creations the church had lied to me about. It was a scare tactic to get people to believe and it seemed to work. Plus, people blaming the Devil for things always gave them a scapegoat to blame for anything from temptation to world hunger. "The Devil made me do it" was a great insanity plea for serial killers on trial.

Yet as far as I could see, no horned creatures ran around luring me toward hell or forcing me to do things. If there was a devil, I wanted to think of him as being about two-feet tall, carrying a trick-or-treat bag, and asking for candy on Halloween. I downplayed Satan.

And the way I saw it, if somehow I was wrong, and he was

real, and those crazy, foaming-at-the-mouth people in church were right, then the Devil and I had a nonaggression treaty. As long as I didn't go out looking for him, he didn't go out looking for me. And plus, he had more important people to worry about, like Billy Graham, the president of the United States, or a host of other saintly folk, but not me.

———

I was not really that excited about the Bible, but to be honest, if I was going to follow this trail that there was a spiritual enemy, I really had nowhere else to turn. And so I started reading the Bible and a few books explaining what the Bible said about evil. I was looking for the Devil. I wanted to learn about him and understand more about all of this spiritual warfare stuff.

I found a lot of verses about evil. The Bible explained that evil's beginning was not found in the depths of hell—breathing fire and plotting destruction—it was in heaven. According to these books and to Scriptures, before the human story began, before Adam and Eve, God created angels—thousands upon thousands of them—to be his servants. Of them all, God raised up three to be the commanders and the captains over all the rest. These three were his closest companions: Lucifer, Gabriel, and Michael.

Apparently these weren't fat little baby cherubim with little bows and arrows fluttering around waiting for Valentine's Day; these guys were fierce, powerful, and strong. Not only that, but they were also glorious and stunning to behold. Of the three, Lucifer was the main guy in rank, power, and splendor. Read this description, which scholars say is of Lucifer at his beginning; it is straight out of the Bible. It completely shocked me.

"You were the model of perfection,
    full of wisdom and perfect in beauty.
You were in Eden,
    the garden of God;
every precious stone adorned you. . . .
You were on the holy mount of God. . . .
You were blameless in your ways.[2]

Although Lucifer was a commander of angels and second only to the Lord of all creation, he was not content with his title and position. I read more of what followed: "Your heart became proud on account of your beauty, and you corrupted your wisdom because of your splendor."[3] Apparently Lucifer was not happy. He wanted more. He wanted the kingdom and throne for himself. He wanted to be God.

Because of this, Lucifer took those in his command and rebelled. The Bible says,

War broke out in Heaven. Michael and his Angels fought the Dragon [Lucifer]. The Dragon and his Angels fought back, but were no match for Michael. They were cleared out of Heaven, not a sign of them left. The great Dragon—ancient Serpent, the one called Devil and Satan, the one who led the whole earth astray—thrown out, and all his Angels thrown out with him, thrown down to earth. . . .

    Helpless with rage, the Dragon raged at the Woman [Eve], then went off to make war with the rest of her children, the children who keep God's commands and hold firm to the witness of Jesus."[4]

This was all shocking to me. Lucifer—aka "the Devil"—was once *good*. He had stood and conducted the choirs in heaven in praising and worshiping God. Apparently he began to covet these praises for himself, caused an uprising, went to war against God, and lost. As a result, Lucifer and the angels that followed him were cast down from heaven to the earth, and now these demon angels and Lucifer had a new, self-appointed mission: if they couldn't get to God, they were hell-bent on destroying God's ultimate creations on earth. Those who reflected his glory, and the ones God created to bear his image—you and me.

Apparently, there is a war going on, and we are in the middle of it.

———

It wasn't until recently, on a road trip with my friend Jesse, that I was really awakened to how evil works. As we traveled across America for a video project, we made our way west and stopped in Las Vegas for the night. I had heard so much about the Las Vegas strip. I had to see it for my own eyes. Although it is called "sin city," there was something fascinating and intriguing about the place, or at least in my mind. As we drove through the barren desert valleys of Nevada at dusk, we saw the lights in the distance. The city was bright, brilliant, and huge. As we got closer, there was so much around us, so much to see and for people to do and experience. From the gambling to the strip clubs to all the bars and restaurants.

Yet looking around, something in me was mesmerized and drawn to it. It might sound like an odd thing to say, but I was drawn to the Las Vegas lights and the wonder of the place. Looking at the massive hotels and bright displays surrounding us, along with other buildings, I realized it was beautiful. The giant structures thousands of feet tall, with billboards and massive television screens covering them and all this stuff going on all around fascinated me.

As we got out of the car and walked around, I noticed that almost every one of the casinos and hotels had a theme. Each casino was some version of a famous building somewhere else in the world — all of them monuments to the greatness of some culture's achievements. There was the Taj Mahal of India, the Pyramid of the Egyptians, Caesar's Palace that looked like a city in Rome, Paris Hotel, which had a huge replica of the Eiffel Tower, and even New York, New York, which was a miniature version of the skyscrapers of the Big Apple.

I couldn't help but wonder, with all the money poured into it, why not something original? Why not a brilliant new architecture marvel? As we kept walking, things hustled all around us. You could easily see into the casinos and the thousands of slot machines where people mindlessly put in money and pulled the levers. I couldn't believe how many people gambled, completely zoned out from reality. I just stopped and watched for a minute.

As I thought about what I saw, I experienced a moment of clarity that I'm pretty sure came from God. Here were all these world-renowned buildings, none of them the original. All of them were copies. And even though they were fakes, they were still beautiful and mesmerizing and appealing. I was still drawn to them.

I wondered if that was how evil had been working in my life for all these years? I thought about the architects, owners, and designers of these Las Vegas buildings. They had spent all this money creating elaborate buildings that were an architectural marvel. They invested millions and millions of dollars to make them look like replicas, so people would come into their casino and spend their money.

Vegas plays with people — their desires and their needs. Desire was everywhere. Even the name *desire* was posted on billboards and huge signs flashing throughout. And yet, few people leave Las Vegas with more than cheap souvenirs. Certainly they had experiences, but none that brought lasting satisfaction. Beauty and weddings and promise abounded, but so did heartbreaks and divorce and great disappointment. As I walked around, it hit me: This was the matrix. A place where people had brought their desires and hopes. It was a place that promised great and big things. From winning money to women. But in the end, it couldn't offer them anything. It was only a copy, and a version of the thing they really wanted.

Isn't that how sin works? It doesn't look awful or bad or ugly. It looks beautiful, charming, and full of promises. Even the fruit back in the garden was "pleasing to the eye, and also desirable for gaining wisdom" (Genesis 3:6). Could sin appeal to our heart's true desire, the desire that originally came from God? Is part of why sin attracts us, or why we enjoy it, because it promises to meet some deep need or ache in our souls?

I realized that is how evil had been working in my life. It was always offering me such a beautiful duplicate of the real thing I wanted, and then luring me into a dark alley or some false version, like a slot machine, to get it.

The fraternity and all my pursuits had promised me a true brotherhood and friendships. Freedom. A chance to find beauty and enter into so much life and adventure. It was promising me so much — the fulfillment of the aches inside of me. But it wasn't giving me the real thing, the God thing — it gave me the copy. A copy that felt good for a while, but never was the real thing. If this was true, then most of my life had been settling for a fake—a version of the things I wanted, but not the real things themselves.

I thought to myself, *What if the Devil was the greatest copy cat?* What if his goal wasn't to take us away from our desires, but to bring us into them and give us the false version of the things we wanted? The Bible even tells us, "Satan himself masquerades as an angel of light."[5] What might it be like to find the true version? Could God actually have the answers to the desires of my heart?

I couldn't believe I was saying it, but I had to believe. Right there on the streets of Las Vegas I realized all this talk about evil was true. Evil was real, and it was charming in its own way, and it had been blinding me, and had blinded all of these people. I had been led into a false version of the things my heart really desired—beauty, strength, success, and friends. Evil was preying on my God-given desires and giving me beautiful and brilliant—but empty—copies instead.

CHAPTER FOUR

the king

"We want a king over us. Then we will be like all the other nations, with a king to lead us and to go out before us and fight our battles."

1 SAMUEL 8:19-20

Before I take you any further in my story, I have to take you back to high school again. I think it was around that time when I started searching for a leader and a guide. Back then, I assumed if I was ever going to become the man I wanted to be, I would have to find a guy living the life I wanted. I needed to find a guy who could guide me.

I wanted to find someone strong, self-confident, and respected by others. I needed a guy who had made it through, and who I could get behind, and who would cut a path through the uncharted lands of high school and into the world beyond. I needed a man who idealized masculinity and could show me "the way."

I think I wanted to find a guy who didn't struggle with normal guy things like I did. He didn't struggle with asking girls out on dates. He didn't have to deal with pimples, or have trouble making the first team in sports, or drive a beat up junk car, or have wimpy biceps, or parents who checked in on him on weekends.

———

The first guy I found to meet this standard was Donnie. He was a senior at my high school. He seemed like the entire package: handsome, athletic, strong, talented with the ladies, and dripping in the masculinity I was looking to find. By the time I noticed him, he was already a legend and a king in the high school halls of Franklin Road Academy. He seemed to have been blessed with everything a man needed to succeed, even a red Toyota pickup truck.

I still remember sitting outside on the school steps with my friends for the annual homecoming high school parade, as the seniors drove by in a caravan of cars decorated with streamers and balloons. They were waving and screaming and honking madly at all the underclassmen. Last in line was Donnie's red pickup. I remember seeing it out of the corner of my eye as it rounded the turn onto our stretch of road. It gleamed in the sun. While everyone else was yelling and screaming to get our attention, Donnie wouldn't think of it. He was calm and collected. There were no streamers or balloons on his truck either. Instead, his decoration was the entire cheerleading team standing in the bed of his truck and waving. As I watched his head tilted back, with one hand on the wheel and Ray-Bans hiding his eyes, I was convinced

Donnie was the guy who had something to teach me about being a man.

———

Before Donnie ever came on the scene, there had been another man I was told was a king. As you know by now, I had heard about Jesus all my life. During my sophomore year of high school, a magician spoke at an assembly and did some tricks, and then talked about God and our need to accept Jesus as Savior and then follow him as King. That day, whether it was the Holy Spirit or this magician's magical spell, something clicked in me, and I raised my hand and recited his instructions to put Jesus in my heart and ask him to forgive me of all my wrongs. Although something happened in my soul that day, there came another problem.

Jesus was no Donnie.

Most kings and men of great influence had star performances, good looks, money, women chasing them, and nice cars or big trucks. The more I read about Jesus, the more I discovered he was not the kind of king I had been looking to follow. He had good stories, but those stories seemed to lack anything to do with me and the struggles I faced daily. Multiplying bread and fish seemed to have little to do with being a man or about this desire in me to date girls. The Good Samaritan reminded people to do good to your neighbor, but didn't answer the questions I had about finding my strength or my search for beauty, or for many of the other relevant things in my life.

Even physically, Jesus seemed to be a bit frail, weak, and less masculine than what I was looking to follow in a king. I was soon questioning whether asking this "king" into my heart had been a good decision.

But apparently Jesus lived in me for good and was not going away. I didn't know what to think of that. I was told I needed him for the salvation of my soul, to be forgiven, and to go to heaven one day, and I believed it. But as I said before, I really wanted him to leave my heart and bother some other kid for a while so I could deal with some of the issues I needed answers for. It wasn't that I didn't want him at all, it was just that I thought it might be better if he skipped my teens and twenties and came back when I was in my thirties and ready to settle down and think more about heaven and my future.

Jesus was a king, but his kingdom seemed to exist in another world, and to be honest, it didn't sound like a place I was ready to follow him into.

When I entered college and joined the fraternity, I still believed in Jesus, but I had actually grown ashamed of him. The further I stepped into the world, the more I avoided any claims he was the King of my heart. The fraternity was a no-man's-land for talking religion and specifically talking about Jesus. My frat brothers seemed to see Jesus as sort of a cross between Mr. Rogers and Mickey Mouse — both somewhat make-believe and phony, but definitely reserved for kids. Although I never said it out loud, I wished God had sent someone a little bit stronger, more masculine, and kingly. I mean, Jesus should have been a stud: tough, powerful, and at least a little bit unpredictable — a guy who fraternity guys would respect, a guy more like Donnie in high school. We needed a rogue, a real fighter, a tough, hardened warrior to follow — a guy like Maximus from *Gladiator*.

We needed a guy who could talk to us about the real things of life and how to cut a path through it.

The fact that Jesus wasn't popular like Donnie or a warrior like Maximus was part of the reason why I had so much conflict in following him. I wanted a leader who could hold his own, and show me the way, and speak to these relevant needs and desires in my heart.

My search for a leader continued through college. And although God was moving deeply in my life, I still had my hopes in finding a man to be my guide. I was finally to get my chance in college. I became roommates with a guy who seemed to have the answers. He was not ordinary like the rest of us. The guy was a beast. His shoulders were the size of bowling balls. He was too big for everything: shirts, shoes, cars, beds, and even rooms. And he also happened to play for the national championship Tennessee football team and, within a year, became a captain. Because of all this, he was also one of the most recognized faces on a campus of 30,000 students. And considering his success, his popularity, and his tough guy image, he was just the sort of leader I was looking to follow.

Chris and I met in class. I was a pretty outgoing guy and needed another roommate, so one day I decided to ask him if he wanted to move in with my friend Matthew and me. He agreed. "The man" was coming to live at our house. "The man" whose name had an hypnotic effect on girls and caused looks of reverence from guys. "The man" was soon to be our roommate, and that was very good news.

I wanted Chris to be my roommate partly because I needed

a roommate for the house I lived in, but mostly because I was looking for a "real man" to guide me still. Of all the guys I had ever met, he seemed to be the best one to follow. I wouldn't have to watch from afar as I had with Donnie; this king was physically strong, popular, had a Tennessee cheerleader as a girlfriend, and when he spoke, his voice boomed like that of a lion—and this guy lived with me.

I hoped that others would associate me with him. Although they never noticed me first, if they stared long enough, and low enough, there I was. Being the guy beside *the guy* had many advantages. It was amazing the immediate respect I felt just from walking into a room with him. Girls, other guys, and even professors would look over and stare.

I worked hard to convince Chris to like me, so most of our time together involved me trying to suck up to him. It required a large amount of energy trying to find things in common that we could talk about. He was everything I wanted to be, and so I didn't have a whole lot in common with him. And although he never seemed to ask much about my world, I really never thought too much about it at the time. I mean, after all, he was a king, and I was just lucky to be living with him—right?

Living with this king, I found out what a king did, what a king thought, and how a king spent his time when he was not on national television taking interviews from reporters or getting phone calls from girls. And, to tell you the truth, he did not live up to my initial expectations. He left food out. He didn't clean his dishes or turn off the lights when he left a room. He never took out the trash. Yet more than any of that, it didn't take long for me to learn that he was insecure, had trouble with women, and struggled to find real friends and things to do on the weekends.

He was a guy a lot like me.

I couldn't believe it, but within two months, I realized he wasn't going to be able to help me because he struggled too. I had wanted him to be a king and do something for me, but he was really just another guy like me who didn't have any more answers than I did. I had hoped by following him, something would turn around for me, but nothing did — except that I found myself doing more housework than I had before.

It all hit me one night when we were out together at a bar. All these people kept looking over at us, and coming up to him, and starting small talk. Their eyes gleamed hoping they could talk with him and maybe be his friend. As I watched, I realized that was me. I had put him on a pedestal and made him into something he could never fulfill. I had asked of him something he could never do for me. I was in need of a guide, and although he was a good man, he didn't have the answers I was looking for because he was looking for them himself.

It was in the middle of all this, and through my struggles to find a guide and seeing my own brokenness, when Jesus came back. And maybe, if I was honest, I really started coming back to him. I had tried everything, putting my hopes in everyone, but all of it was coming up dry and empty. Nothing worked. I mean nothing. I had put my hopes in everything from beer to women to a big football player, and none of it gave me what I had hoped for.

I believe this new conversation with Jesus really started when I had run out of options. I found myself driving down to the Tennessee River in the pitch darkness over many late nights trying to find a peaceful place to sort through all this. I remember sitting for hours on the rocks overlooking the river and the city lights, sometimes angry and sometimes crying. I did this over years.

Even in the midst of the parties that seemed like the place to be, I felt called back down that road, and to those rocks by the river, alone. I had never before allowed myself to sit alone, nor had I ever driven to a place to find solitude, or created space for God, but the weird part was I didn't feel alone there.

I would stare out at the darkness and the lights reflecting off the river, rolling over all these questions and things going on in my head. It usually started with my frustrations, and really my anger, much of it directed toward God.

Over a period of months, I started to feel more alone at the parties, even with everyone screaming and laughing, than I did next to this river on a Friday night all by myself with my Bible. I had no idea what was happening to me.

One night during this time of questioning and mumbling that was part anger and part prayer, Jesus simply answered. I can't explain it really. It's not like I heard voices or anything, or that I had a vision of angels. I continued to realize that my life and how I had tried to make it happen wasn't working. I could not pick it up and make it into anything. I couldn't create someone or become something or date a girl who would make all of this go away. All things began to merge into one. I was a broken man. A broken man who needed help and who was hiding. I did not have answers, and I did not have a guide to give me those answers.

That river is where something cut through all my hiding and began comforting me and holding me right in the middle of all the mess. I just sat there and soaked it in and let it fall on my face and in my heart, and let it wash over me. All I did was show up. It was so mysterious, but at the same time refreshing and healing. It was real.

I felt like someone was there, talking back through the pages of Scripture. And I was actually listening and allowing the words to do something and even guide my heart. I had prayed before, and had moments of sensing God, but never before had that sensation been as personal and intimate as this.

Despite how dark and fearful and confusing everything was, I felt myself being wrapped up each night and protected. Although it was no great overnight conversion, or specific moment-in-time turnaround, or a raised hand in a church service, or an act of total repentance after which I never stumbled or questioned again, I found that through my wrestling with God, and over my frustrations, my anger, and even my going down to the river, I was believing in God and even Jesus again. I was reading his words in the Bible and actually listening and even following them. Although I had never planned it, or even wanted it at the time, the same guy I had written off, and was a bit ashamed of, was somehow entering back into my life in a fresh and real way.

It was during the time of these late nights on the river when I met an older man named Rick who began a Bible study in the fraternity. One day in our small group of guys, Rick read a passage from Revelation that would shine a light on a Jesus I had never seen before. Rick explained it was when Jesus comes back to claim his throne on earth during the Second Coming.

I saw heaven standing open and there before me was a white horse, whose rider is called Faithful and True. With justice he judges and makes war. His eyes are like blazing fire, and on his head are many crowns. He has a name written on him that no one knows but he himself. He is dressed in a robe dipped in blood, and his name is the Word of God. The armies of heaven were following him, riding on white horses and dressed in fine linen, white and clean. Out of his mouth comes a sharp sword with which to strike down the nations. "He will rule them with an iron scepter." He treads the winepress of the fury of the wrath of God Almighty. On his robe and on his thigh he has this name written:

KING OF KINGS AND LORD OF LORDS.[1]

My first reaction was: "This was *Jesus*? Really?" I couldn't believe it. Are we talking about the same Jesus who told stories about sheep and bread and hung out with children on his lap? Talk about a transformation! *A sword out of his mouth . . . his robe dipped in blood . . . and an army of angels?* Imagine that guy walking through the hallways at the frat house? Think people would listen to what he had to say? Definitely. Think people would be laughing then? Yeah, right.

This was no mild Jesus bouncing babies on his knee. He was no little lamb. This was a physical specimen that people would notice as a true king. He was *It*—he oozed with masculinity. He embodied it. This guy would get respect from all people. No more feeling embarrassed about carrying your Bible around, or little smirks from people in school who thought Christianity was for the weak.

But my second reaction to the passage was more anger. Up to this point, my conversations with Jesus focused on him as a comforter and a kind man who understood me and my heartache. Talking to Jesus, I still had images of sheep and little children in my head. Why hadn't he shown up in all his power like this the first time? Coming like this would have convinced everyone I knew that Jesus was real, tough, and completely untamable. I probably would have noticed him, back on that pew, and not dreamt about being somewhere else. Things would have been less complicated. People would have listened—*I* would have listened—and obeyed in high school. He would have had my allegiance and respect. This was a man with authority, power, and strength. This was a leader and someone who commanded respect and wielded intimidation. This was what I wanted to follow. This guy. This *Jesus*.

Yes, yes, yes.

But why did he choose to show up as the "other" Jesus? If you are God, why not lay down the law, prove yourself, and show your kingdom by flexing your stuff and showing it off? Why didn't he show up in a way that his very presence would have showed everyone who he really was? It didn't make sense—why the two different and almost opposite versions of Jesus?

I read a quote one day from C.S. Lewis: "Christianity is the story of how earth's rightful King has landed here in disguise and is calling on his people to join him in a grand campaign of sabotage."[2]

Sabotage? Jesus coming in disguise?

It had me thinking. Had that been God's plan all along? When Jesus walked this earth, he was plain—you could almost say "normal," or at least he was for the first thirty years of his life. He had nothing of the appearance of a great king, or nobleman, let alone the Son of God. He just didn't look the part. He certainly didn't have the crown or jewels or palaces or respect of a king. Had he done all of this on purpose?

I remembered that the Old Testament gives hundreds of prophecies about how Jesus would come. These prophecies said he would be born in Bethlehem[3] and that he would come into Jerusalem "gentle and riding on a donkey."[4] It was as if the way Jesus appeared, lived, and died were all part of God's plan. Even a verse in Scripture says, "He had no beauty or majesty to attract us to him."[5] It was as if God didn't want Jesus to appear as a conquering king, but instead disguised as a humble story-teller, teacher, and miracle worker.

If the Bible predicted that Jesus would come like this, then it must have been God's plan. I wondered if God had taken all the external things away on purpose. He had stripped Jesus of all that would make him seem a king so people wouldn't get into him because of his looks or performance, like so many people do with celebrities, athletes, and political leaders. Instead, Jesus had everything on the inside. I wondered if his strength, power, and authority had been there from the beginning, but he just didn't use these for his own gain. Instead of using them to wow people and get respect, he laid all of that aside so he could do what his Father had sent him to the earth to do—nothing more, nothing less.

If Jesus had come to earth the first time as Revelation described him, he probably knew we would be fascinated with all his external power, glory, and beauty. We wouldn't even care about what he said or who he was. We would just want pictures of him standing with his sword before his army of angels. We would want to be seen out with him at public places. If God didn't clothe Jesus in riches and gold, weaponry and celebrity status, it was because he knew people would flock to him because of that, and not because of what he taught or what he said or what he did.

Jesus was born in a small town, to a small-town woman. His birth wasn't in a palace or with great wealth and trumpets sounding. He was rejected in the inn and born in a barn. He grew up learning to be a carpenter — a simple craftsman — not a soldier, a politician, or anything close to a king. He could have had it all, but instead he rejected it all, and stripped everything the world would praise him for, so he could relate to us, and then save us. He was not forced into dying; he chose to lay his life down. He chose the cross and to throw off all his grandeur and power and glory so he could become like us — to show his love and the true fulfillment of our hearts' desires.

I had never thought of it that way before. It was the ultimate act of love and humility. He chose to shed those things great and mighty to show something greater and let his life and his actions and the cross teach us something more than fawning over his looks would have. All my life, I had been more impressed by worldly kings and those guys around me than I had ever been by Jesus. It was amazing: the things that had turned me away from Jesus all those years, began to be the things I respected most about him. He chose to take the form of a servant. He gave up power, respect, fortune, and sitting at the right hand of God to humble himself as a man to serve us, die for our sins, and bring the power of God back into our lives. He was about restoring these things. And he wanted his words and teachings to be our guide and nothing else.

In all my searching, I had come full circle. He was the King everyone needed and was looking for. He was the true man of strength, of wisdom, of power, and of authority, but he chose to fly under the world's radar so the world did not recognize him. His dying on the cross caught the world by complete surprise.

God wasn't found in the flashy and fake. He was in the simple and beautiful. He wasn't in the counterfeits; he was in the *real*. And where the world offered shortcuts to distract us and gave us false answers to our desires, God's ways had never changed since the day he created the earth. He knew more about fulfilling those desires than the world did, and he wanted us to pay attention to those ways and words above all the glamour, the riches, the power, the victories, and the temporary success and satisfactions the world offered us.

After years of searching, I realized Jesus was the King I wanted — the King I had been looking for all those nights, and in people. And despite how weird some religious people were about him, and all the things that had turned me away, I was proud to admit that Jesus really was the true King of my heart.

the brotherhood

*How good and pleasant it is when brothers
live together in unity!*

PSALM 133:1

It was the last day of "Hell Week," our initiation into the fraternity, and I was dripping wet, cold, exhausted from exertion
and too-little sleep. I also had a blindfold over my eyes. It was
early—probably somewhere around 4 a.m. —when the voice
I had been hoping to hear finally rang out from down the hall:
"Alexander Hood, come with us."

It was a great relief. After months of being a pledge, proving myself worthy to be a member, and finally after this week
of hell, they called my name. Like each guy before me, I was
escorted blindfolded into the chapter room and into a ceremony of becoming a brother, which until this point, had been
shrouded in mystery.

As they began the secret rituals of initiation into the bonds of the frat, I realized I had entered into the place that seemed to hold the answers for some of the questions of my heart and my desire to find a brotherhood. After the secret ceremony, as the blindfold was removed, I rose up to discover the entire fraternity surrounding me. They greeted me with hugs and cheers, welcoming me into the bonds of their brotherhood.

It was a moment I had been waiting for my entire life.

I had always wanted to be a part of an exclusive band of guys. It had started when I was running through those wildlands of Ohio as a boy with the neighborhood kids, camping out with the guys at a friend's farm on the weekends, or competing together in fall soccer leagues and other sports. There was something about being together in those moments. There was a camaraderie and brotherhood and connection with other guys, sharing, laughing, striving, and living.

My first real sense of this camaraderie was in fourth grade when the Bowser Club formed. It was created by four guys who, at ten, were the movers and shakers of our school. They were the guys who made things happen. They cut membership cards out of notebook paper, used yellow highlighter over pen for effect, and clear tape to laminate them. Across the front, in big highlighted letters, they wrote "The Bowser Club." Then they put it in their Velcro wallets and flashed them to the rest of us like they were the FBI.

I was willing to do anything to be part of it. I needed what those guys had. The four guys who created it gathered during recess to have their "secret" meetings where everyone else could see. I remember looking on with the other guys as we pretended to play football. We were really dreaming of having our own tape-laminated Bowser cards and sitting with them on those steps. We had no idea what they were doing or talking about, which only fed our passion to be "in." But it wasn't up to us; you couldn't join unless the four guys voted you in. I wondered for days, was I Bowser Club material? I had my doubts. But a week later the response came back, "Yes." The card was given to me in a secret ceremony. At the next recess, I sat and looked from those steps at all the losers playing football.

Although I was now part of *the* guys, I soon found there wasn't much to the Bowser Club besides having one of the cards and sitting on the steps during recess. The whole point was to say we were better than the rest of the guys. And it had worked. In fact, it worked too well. It really tore kids up not to be picked for membership. But we didn't care. We wanted it to stay small and exclusive.

Eventually feelings were hurt. Guys went home crying because they had been told they couldn't be in the club. Then finally one mom got so fed up she called the school and talked with the principal. The next day, she disbanded the Bowser Club. The teachers raided our desks and wallets and seized our cards like it was a drug bust.

———

Why did I sign up to be hazed and go through so much hell? Well, the fraternity seemed to offer what the Bowser Club and sports and other clubs had attempted to offer—a group of guys that bonded together against the rest of the world. I can remember the day after my second week of college as I walked from my dorm room to the frat house to accept my bid as one of their pledges and begin the whole process. Approaching the house, I saw the entire brotherhood gathered on the porch as they waited on me to come up the steps. They greeted me with cheers as I pledged my loyalty to the house. It was a powerful feeling being wanted by guys that badly.

The day I signed the pledge card, I sat down with the other forty-five guys in my pledge class, and the rush chairmen spoke to us: "Guys, I want you to look around this room. These are the guys who will be your best friends *for life*. They are your new brothers. They will be at your wedding and at your funeral and many of the other important points in between. Welcome to our brotherhood."

Those words stuck with me — and I stuck to them.

———

The fraternity was not the only or first place I learned that I had brothers and was offered fellowship. Sitting in a church pew, I had been told that the people around me were my "brothers and sisters in Christ." Although my family never went, every Wednesday evening, church parking lots would fill up for fellowship suppers. But these were not like the gatherings of "The Fellowship of the Ring" — it was more "The Fellowship of the Green Bean Casserole." Although I never actually joined the suppers to verify this, I knew enough by watching the old people and their walkers get out of their cars with their side dishes. Attending these kinds of meetings never rang very true to my desires for being part of a band of brothers.

For them, this might have been good fellowship, but I needed more. I wanted to live for something and be a part of something big. I was convinced their conversations were about as wide as cousin Jimmy and his tattoo, and deep as comments on prayer in school. I was never very motivated to walk into church to fulfill this longing for brotherhood inside me. I was not convinced at the time God had much to say about it. The glimpses I had of Bible studies did not speak as much as the desire and connection I found in sports or out on a Friday night with my friends. Church fellowship appeared as dry and old as week-old bread. I would pass on the potato salad and chose the fraternity instead.

The first thing the fraternity gave us—the forty-five new pledges—was a retreat in the Smoky Mountains. No other brothers, just the new guys. They wanted us to get to know each other and bond in the rugged beauty. I was pretty nervous about the weekend. I wanted this brotherhood, but just because I did, didn't mean I wasn't still frightened of this new group. To be honest, I had learned to be afraid of guy relationships—afraid of being honest and real and opening my heart with other guys. Fear played a huge role in my life, especially when sharing my heart with guys. I didn't want other guys to see my weaknesses or see through my masks. How would I fit in? How would I relate to them? Would they like me? Or would they see right through me and find nothing worthwhile?

I was intimidated. I didn't know most of these guys. And these were not the dorks no one else wanted to hang out with—they were the popular, athletic, and social kings of their high schools. They were an intimidating bunch of guys—a bunch of guys I wanted to fit in with, but wasn't sure I measured up to.

We arrived, unpacked, and spread ourselves and our stuff

throughout the place, claiming beds and floor space for the night, and then tapping the kegs. I had never seen so much beer flow so freely in one place before in my life. We fired up the grills, turned on the television, and drank beer like it was water. We started at sunup, and it lasted well past sundown. We goofed off, played music, clogged the hot tub with Cheetos, and drank until we couldn't see straight.

I think everyone drank so much because of what we heard was going to happen that night. A brother had told a few guys outside the house before we left: "Be prepared for the candle ceremony. A candle is passed around with the lights off, and each of you will get a chance to tell your story. You get to tell everyone what your life has been like. The real parts. The honest parts. It's how you get to know each other—the good and the bad."

The rumors spread about that conversation, and as it came closer you could almost smell the fear—fear of honestly sharing ourselves and telling others about the hurts, pains, and tragedies of our lives, the stuff we had locked away for years. I think we drank in hopes it would give us the courage to be honest about our lives to these complete strangers.

Somewhere in the dark of the evening, and when the beer was running out, the candle was lit.

We sat for hours—it seemed an eternity—as the candle was slowly passed and each guy opened up his heart and talked about his life. The guys told story after story of tragedy, disappointment, and heartache. The toughest, hardest, wildest, and biggest of us broke down sobbing uncontrollably as they opened up their wounds. They told of broken homes, sexual abuse, abandonment, betrayal, death, and pain.

It seemed as if every kind of life-reshaping tragedy possible had happened to one or another of us. Never had guys been so vulnerable and honest around me.

That night I felt something I had never truly felt. I realized I was not alone. I never knew other guys had those kinds of stories to tell. They looked like guys who had it all—captains of their high school football team, the ones people looked up to and respected as leaders—and yet, those were the guys who, after a few beers, freely opened up about the pain, tears, and hurt inside. I realized every one of us, every guy, had been wounded and hurt. Life had broken us all. We all had pain from struggles and tragedies. I also realized that most of us had spent our entire lives holding it in, scared and ashamed of ever sharing it, believing guys don't talk about that kind of stuff.

As we left those mountains the next morning, leaving the empty kegs and clutter, things were different. Something had happened in those mountains and over that candle and with those guys. The strangers now had names and stories that I remembered. It felt more true and real than anything I had ever known before. As we wove back through the mountains to the University of Tennessee and to our fraternity house, I knew I had found a fellowship of guys I could live with as a family. We were brothers.

As the months continued, we grew closer as a pledge class and as we sat as one entire section in the stadium with the other frat brothers, screaming and yelling together as Tennessee strove for a national football championship. During homecoming week, we decorated our float, laughing and drinking together for what seemed like 196 hours straight. We worked together on interfraternity competitions, spending so many late nights living the high fraternity life. Practically every day we would swap stories at the lunch table about the night before, laughing. We might study together in the library, carry someone home who was too drunk to walk, defend each other in fights, or share a meal at 1 a.m. after a party. It was incredible the feeling of strolling into a bar to find ten of your brothers already there, or walking into class with a bunch of them, or seeing them all over the campus. We truly loved each other like brothers. There is no better way to put it and nothing weird about it.

It was actually the truest thing I had ever found, but also, as I eventually learned while gazing into that mirror and the many nights on the Tennessee River, it was still not what I was really looking for. It was the closest thing I had ever found to actually fulfilling my desire for brotherhood, but it was still somehow incomplete.

I realized that despite the brotherhood I had found in the fraternity, it had nothing to do with God. In fact, most of our time was spent sinning. And yet, what made it so hard was, I still believed the fraternity had a truer form of brotherhood than I had ever experienced in church. The camaraderie of a frat party still seemed truer to the call of my heart for fellowship than a church service or Bible study ever had. It was a very confusing time for me.

But I also knew there was something very wrong with all of this. Was it my desire for this kind of brotherhood that was wrong, or had we lost something in the church that the fraternities had found? Could I really follow Jesus and still have this kind of brotherhood, or did I have to give one up to have the other?

The more I explored this, the more God revealed, little by little. The issue wasn't our friendship and our commitment to one another, it was our cause. We really didn't serve anything greater than ourselves or for a party. We lived for the moment. We never had a mission greater than being friends, drinking beer, finding girls, or competing against a rival fraternity. We had a brotherhood, *but a brotherhood of what?* I began asking myself. *What are we living for? What purpose do we serve? What mission are we on?*

If this wasn't it, what else was there? Was it better to ignore such questions and just enjoy the time we had together? Or shut out this desire for more? Although there were ideals and oaths of the fraternity, it seemed strikingly similar to the Bowser Club—an exclusive group of guys that didn't have much to serve other than ourselves.

I eventually joined a small group that met weekly in a dorm room to read through the Scriptures and talk. It was very different than what I had first thought about church fellowship, and I actually enjoyed it. There was no green bean casserole. I was eager to read and pray and find God with other guys. I really was hungry to seek God and understand more about Jesus. For the first time I was tasting what the true community of God's people could be. We talked about God and Jesus and stepped into Scripture in a new way. We were hearing truth and sitting under the Word of God and being taught.

I was around godly guys, and the way I saw it, this study was a part of the real brotherhood God wanted to bring me. As you can imagine, the guys around the frat house were not very supportive. They gave me a hard time about going to all these "God things." Only a few semesters before, I was the social chairman of the pledge class and announcing our next parties, and now I had betrayed them and found a new group. Rumors were floating around that I was "getting religious." They started giving me nicknames.

They said I had joined "The God Squad."

So I stopped hanging out at the frat as much. And as my life was turning around, I didn't spend nights out drinking with them or partying like I used to. Slowly the gap widened to the point I was barely even considered a brother anymore. No phone calls and no more time hanging out. Suddenly, the brotherhood I had grown close to, that I had hoped would meet the needs inside of me for friendship, was being left behind.

Then one night something strange happened. I knew something was up when I walked into the frat house after the Bible study and felt myself grow jealous when I saw the guys hanging out, playing pool, and drinking beer together. And this kept happening. I would come by the house to eat lunch and see everyone was sharing life together, joking around on the steps, telling stories about the night before, laughing, and enjoying one another—everyone except me, that is.

I remember sitting on the porch one evening after dinner feeling so alone. I had mixed feelings because I wanted to follow God, but I also wanted to be back in there among the guys doing whatever they were doing. I wanted to be in the middle of those parties, drinking beer, bonding, and laughing with them. They had something that was so true about brotherhood that I realized I didn't find with the Bible study guys. I knew the truth, but I still wanted to hang out with the frat guys. I wanted something more. It wasn't about the booze; it was about belonging in a band of brothers that knew and loved each other.

In our Bible study, I was learning a lot about God and

Scripture, but our times together never got personal and raw. There was a pursuit of knowledge, doctrine, and scriptural answers to the big questions of life, but there was no real brotherhood or fellowship among us. I never saw any of those guys outside of the Bible study. We never spent time *living* together — working, laughing, joking, or even crying together like I'd had with the guys at the frat house. It felt more like a history class. No one was really opening up or confessing sins and struggles. We had some lofty prayers, but in all those meetings no one was really offering their personal stories, or even what they were facing in their daily lives.

Even though as Christians we should have had the "true brotherhood of God," nothing we had ever done together had come anywhere close to the candle light ceremony in the mountains I had experienced with my pledge class or a night out on the town. We didn't get together on Monday night to play pool, or on Wednesday night for supper, or tailgate together before football games, or even just sit a bit before the study to share life together. We just read the Bible and talked. Don't get me wrong, this was a great thing to do, and I really got a lot from it, but was it enough? Did I really have to give up the other fulfilling aspects of brotherhood to be a Christian?

During that time, I was reading a lot of Scripture on my own as well. I marked up my Bible with highlighters and wrote comments or questions in the margins. I began to notice things I hadn't before — and things specific to this ache inside me. The first thing I noticed was the friendship David had with Jonathan and his mighty men, then the relationship Jesus had with his disciples. The book of Acts said the early Christians "were together and had everything in common"[1] and "broke bread in their homes and ate together with glad and sincere hearts."[2] In other words, they lived and shared life together. I wondered, what life was like back then?

The fellowship of the Bible was not about people hanging out playing church bingo, or eating potato salad at the fellowship supper, or talking about cousin Jimmy and whether or not he would ever turn from his wild ways. And it was not just people sitting around being spiritual and discussing theological positions. Not even close. It looked more like men fighting in a war together. In fact, it looked more like the fellowship I had lived in the fraternity than I could ever have imagined, except that those in the Bible were living for God and enlarging his kingdom, and not just for themselves and their desires to drink, party, and carouse.

This process was pretty gradual and happened over months, but I continued to read on into the New Testament and about the closeness and vulnerability Jesus had with his twelve disciples, and especially John, James, and Peter. Here were thirteen guys doing everything together. They ate together, slept in the same places, and lived their lives as one, just as I had with my brothers during my first two years in the fraternity. There was mission, purpose, and connection behind it all. There was this sense of unity and willingness to lay their lives down for the cause of Christ and their war against evil. There was camaraderie, a connection, and a tremendous sense of community because of this shared mission.

My heart ached as I read this. I had none of that — nothing even close. If this was possible to achieve as the Bible seemed to say it was, then where was I going to find it? Where were guys walking in this kind of brotherhood today? Could this still be achieved?

Here was what I had been looking for all this time, but it still seemed so far away. I felt more desperate than ever for it. I think my ache and my deep need to find this took me out searching, even though I didn't have much of a clue where to begin. I just knew I was searching for something more — something similar to the fraternity, but so much more — more of God, more of each other, more transparent and honest. Simply something more true in every sense of the word.

After I graduated from college, I found myself out of any Bible study or fraternity setting. It was a real wake-up call. It was probably the loneliest point in my life. But out of it, I started to speak this need and desire over the course of the next three or four months with a few friends I had met along the way.

We would sit over a cup of coffee, or eating lunch, or at the friend's house or apartment, and I would just share my thoughts. I asked other guys about their desires for this, and I listened to their experiences, their frustrations, and their thoughts and opinions on the matter.

It was incredible because, as I opened up, I heard the same things going on in their lives that were happening in mine. They had friends they hung out with on the weekends and went to church with, but no one they were really honest with, who they could trust and reveal their full lives and stories with. It seemed there were a lot of guys with a desire for more, but they had nowhere to go for it. They also seemed a bit embarrassed at their aches for this, just as I had been. Ashamed to be a guy and want to hang out with other guys and have this kind of openness.

Different friends all seemed to say the same things: "Are guys supposed to want this? It feels almost wrong. Like guys aren't supposed to have these kinds of relationships with each other. I mean, we're not gay, but does that mean we can't have tight-knit friendships with other guys? Are we really supposed to handle all of this all by ourselves all of the time?" It was crazy, because the more I stepped out of my fears and opened up and was honest with my own feelings in this area, the more other guys admitted they wanted the same thing.

So I started asking them if they wanted to step into more and be part of something, even though I didn't know what it would look like. I asked if they wanted to be part of a group to share more together—from our thoughts about Scripture, to the callings of our hearts, to our prayers and our stories, and the stuff of our lives. Then came another conversation, and another, and before long there were five of us with the same desire, and ache: Ben, Jonathan, Sherman, Jason, and myself.

So I invited them to my place. It was even crazier because none of them even knew each other. They all came over; we cooked some steaks on the grill, and talked. It wasn't forced, and nothing was planned, but the guys just started sharing—and kept sharing.

Four hours later it was midnight, and we were still on the porch, still talking. Five guys who had just met were revealing stories about our lives and our struggles, and laughing. We closed the evening praying together and asked Jesus to come into the places and stories we had shared. And then everyone went home.

I was floored. It had happened. There was something deeper

in that one night than I had shared with any other guys my whole life. And it had all been under God, for his kingdom, and we didn't even have to get drunk to do it.

I was ecstatic. It was the most life-giving fellowship I had ever tasted. We had connected to something deep and raw and real. We had shared and been vulnerable, and unlike that night with the fraternity over the candle, we continued to open up about our lives and our struggles and our joys and our hurts. We had found hope.

We continued to meet as friends and brothers. It wasn't like most groups I had been in, where I felt like I needed to compete to have the most wisdom to offer the rest of the group, or even to pray the best prayer. It had nothing to do with that. We weren't fighting to prove the other wrong or look more spiritual. We were just all willing to admit we were searching for more in life and to encourage one another as well as share our own failures in that pursuit and call out the strengths we saw in each other. We weren't threatened by each other — probably because we were all admitting our brokenness and our need for God. With my old friends in the frat and in high school, we used to make fun of each other and put each other down to make ourselves look better, but in this group we wanted to encourage and call out the strengths we saw in each other.

We kept meeting. We didn't fake our spirituality; instead we confessed our sins, our struggles, our concerns, and shared our victories. When we prayed for one another, and as we read and lived out Scripture, God simply showed up — again and again. It was incredible. We wanted more: more of God and more of each other, so we started spending time together outside our weekly meetings as well. We didn't even do it because it was the Christian thing to do; we did it because our lives and souls depended on it.

I don't want to pretend it was perfect, but each time we met, I felt a new strength in my heart. I was not alone in my battles or temptations anymore. I was not hiding parts of my life from the world nor was I ashamed of who I was on the inside or afraid someone would discover the real me. Nor was there anything unnatural or weird about this connection I wanted with other guys. I had simply found others who were on this journey, who were encouraging me and strengthening me. Guys were now standing beside me. Even during the week, I felt the presence of that group with me, helping me be the man I felt called to be.

But here is the hard part. Some years after graduating, I did what most people do after college: I got married, and we decided to move to a new city. Over a year ago, we packed up the U-Haul with all of our stuff and headed west out of Knoxville toward Colorado.

Although I was eager to start a new life with my wife, moving meant I had to leave behind these new brothers — guys who I was really just getting to know. It was so hard to leave what we had really just begun to enter into together.

Today, I am in a new place, and I am looking for this brotherhood again. I am having to start all over: meeting new guys, talking again about the desires of my new stage of life, testing to see if they are going through the same things, and seeing if I can find a new fellowship of guys to hook up with like the one I had left in Tennessee. I won't lie; it has not been easy. I am facing the same fears again of having to open up and share and find guys who want something deeper, and yet who can play and laugh and get rowdy together. It's not easy to find close friendships. I have been in Colorado over a year, and so far, I have made two good friends.

But after tasting that friendship with those guys back in Tennessee, it has only increased my ache all the more to form another group like it, and I just can't settle for anything less. I am actually hoping there is even more. Thinking about this desire, I wrote the following in my journal the other day:

I am looking for guys who want to know me, and a place where I can get to know guys. I want to feel safe and to be able to trust those guys to share my story, my past, and for others to see there is a purpose behind my life — that there is a weight to my life, and they want to help me come into the fullness of it.

I want it to be a fellowship that doesn't meet because it is the Christian thing to do, or to feel good about it, or to just study the Bible, but because it is necessary for survival in this world. I need to find other guys who have my back while I have theirs. That it is life and death. I am looking for brothers who desire to find companions, fellow soldiers who are on the battlefield serving and who are prepared to live and die for this cause of Christ.

I want to find men who have been fired upon, who have been through trials and suffering, but are stronger and walk closer to God because of it. I want to walk with brothers who are not afraid to ask me tough questions, reveal their own weaknesses, and walk in true strength. I want to find friends that want more from life and friendship. Guys who don't settle for an hour study, or a short conversation, but want more. And want to ultimately walk in truth, and with Jesus, and live and die for this purpose that is so much greater than just ourselves.

beauty

Your vibrant beauty has gotten inside us.

PSALM 89:17, MSG

I remember in kindergarten being huddled up with several other guys on a wooden platform of our playground. We had something important to discuss. Our conversation was regarding our current enemies — girls — and rumors of an airborne infection they were spreading to all of us. The meeting was to remind each other that girls had "cooties," and contact was to be avoided at all costs.

There was indeed something different about girls, and a disease seemed as good an explanation as any. So I did my best to stay away from all of them, which meant no talking, no playing, no touching, no sharing a lunch table.

But all that would soon change.

One day, in second grade, as I sat unsuspectingly in the cafeteria enjoying my lunch, something struck me from across the room. It was not food or a spitball, but the light and glorious presence of one of these disease-infected girls. As Lindsay Lane sat eating her lunch, I noticed her smooth skin, freckles, and silky brown hair. Her smile and face had broken through every barrier and defense boyhood had built into me. A desire called to me, and I took notice. At eight years old, Lindsay had stirred something new in me, something fresh, alive, and real — *beauty*.

From early on, I knew I was not alone in my search for beauty. It seemed to be universal, desired by all — men and women, mothers and children, and even grandparents. It seemed everyone was trying to capture it in some form or another through a camera, by drawing it, writing about it, or by hiking to remote areas to find it. Some people were heading into the Rockies to be surrounded by it or traveling to the ocean hoping to catch a glimpse of it in a sunset.

I had always enjoyed things of beauty. I love the ocean at night, sunrises, and walking through Smoky Mountain National Park. There was even a painting or two that I liked. But while many people seemed content to look at a painting or take a vacation, I was growing much more interested in the beauty sitting next to me in class, who had long hair, who talked and smiled. There was something in that beauty that no sunset or painting could ever equal, or at least not for me.

This longing for beauty brought me to my first obsession with a girl — Deanna (you might remember her from the first chapter). Deanna walked through the door the first day of my freshman year in high school as the new girl in town. She was stunning, charming, and mysterious to all of us. Just like every new girl who came to school, the hallways began buzzing with her name. Guys were drooling, and everyone was talking about who was going to date her.

We were all thinking the same thing: *Who would be the first to ask her out? Who would she like? Who would she date? Who was going to get the girl? Who would be her first boyfriend?*

In high school, if a guy could win the heart of a beautiful girl, it meant something. It had magical power to transform a guy. The guy who could find and hold onto the prettiest girl won a type of validation, his social stock went up a few points, and he stepped up to a whole new level of manhood. I wanted to date Deanna not just because she was easy on the eyes, but because it would bring me respect from other guys and prove I was a real man. I was sure that winning a girl would change me from a confused, fearful boy into a confident and capable man.

———

But I did not appear to have what a girl of this caliber needed. Deanna was snagged by a senior, and I began the long-running experience of watching the girls I had set my sights on date other guys. The best I could do was dream from a distance. Sadly, this became my story. I could never land the girl I wanted to go out with. Sure, I could have dated a girl or two, but not the ones I wanted. I wanted to win "the beauty," but it didn't take long to figure out that these girls weren't interested in a guy like me. So it became my job to convince at least one of them that I was worth her time. And if I could convince her that I was man enough for her to go out with, then maybe I could also convince myself.

But I wasn't very good at that either, and I collected a lot of rejections. Each rejection brought with it questions. *Did I even have something that girls wanted? Would I ever be man enough that they would choose me rather than someone else? How could I get them to notice and like me? Why did it seem so easy for other guys, but not me?*

—————

I took all of these questions home with me each night after school, alone. And with this desire and stirring for beauty, I found a way to taste, for a brief moment, what it might be like to be with *the* beautiful girl. In my fantasies, I got the girl every time. I was her hero and knight in shining armor.

These women would never say "no" to me. This new discovery took me to surfing the Internet and grabbing magazines filled with other women to fantasize about. I went searching through pages and pages of websites looking for the perfect size and face to expose me to new levels of beauty, and then, using my own imagination, I would again sweep beauty off her feet. Pornography offered to fulfill the longing and ache I had inside of me for a woman, and for beauty. This collection of images filled my thought life more and more. Whatever was innocently awakened by Lindsay Lane in second grade had turned into an addiction and an obsession.

Even from the beginning, something in me felt odd and shameful when I looked at porn. I knew it was wrong. But once I'd stepped into that world, I couldn't pull my eyes away. There was something powerful, and something I desired in this form of beauty, that kept me coming back to it in secret. The guilt and conviction was there, but in the midst of the guilt, I would promise myself—and eventually God—I would never do that again. Yet no matter how ashamed I felt, the temptation kept coming back again and again, and I almost always gave in to it.

In college, a new hope arose in me that I could find a real version of the beauty I was searching for online and in magazines. My freshman year, *Playboy* had named the University of Tennessee as one of the most beautiful campuses in the nation. As I walked to class each day, it was not hard to see why — beautiful girls were everywhere.

It was amazing. Beauty flowed through the streets and into the classrooms. It wasn't like high school where there were only a few good-looking girls. Here, they were everywhere. You couldn't walk to class and not see several, or walk down the hallways and not brush up against at least one. With 30,000 students on campus, that also meant roughly 15,000 new girls, and with so many of them so beautiful, I was sure my odds of snagging one were much better.

I finally had my chance. With my new frat brothers, and beer to take off the edge and my fear of rejection, I was ready to step back into my longing and find a girl for myself. The fraternity happened to be the ultimate place to meet girls. Through our functions with the sororities, we had exclusive access to some of the most beautiful girls on campus. We called them "mixers" — parties where one entire sorority would come over to our house to "mix" just with us and drink as much alcohol as we could get them to drink. These parties usually started with dozens of guys standing in a circle, nervous and a bit awkward, pretty much the same as a junior high dance. The girls would walk over to the frat house and gather together on the other side of the room, while the guys were scanning for the "hot ones." We would finally break the ice by handing out drinks. Soon this liquid courage would be flowing freely. Then the real "mixing" would get started on the dance floor, standing along the edges, on the couches in the front room, and eventually — if a guy were "lucky" — up in the individual rooms of the house.

With around thirty-seven guys standing together, though, the question always arose of who was going to get *the* girl — the one that caught the eye of every guy the minute she walked in the door. With so many beautiful women on campus, there were always two or three like this at every mixer — the ones standing out above all the rest. For us frat guys, hooking up with one of them was a competition almost as intense as playing football. Who would be the first to have the nerve to go up and talk with the most beautiful girl at the party? Would he be able to get her to dance with him? Could he keep her laughing and intrigued enough to keep her talking with him and then want to start looking for a place a little more private to hang out? Would he then be able to convince her to come home with him or to his dorm room? And then, after all that delicate work, would he "score"? If he did, he was the guy the others talked about at lunch the next day. He was the guy who had the story to tell that all of the others would listen to in rapt wonder.

I found after breaking through my initial fears, I could do this. I found some girls interested in me, once I made the initial moves. The more mixers we had, the more girls I met. With some beer, I found enough courage to take the risk and mix and mingle and often find a girl by the end of the night.

For most guys, as soon as they got the girl, they lost interest and were on to the next one. And then, at the next party, it was on to the next girl and the next "conquest." I began to notice this same tendency in me. Looking back, I think it wasn't about the girl as much as it was about proving to both myself and my friends that I had what it took to win her for a night. Proving I was a man.

———

This life was not as fulfilling as I had thought it would be either. In fact, it was very similar to my time with pornography. There was an emptiness I felt afterwards. As I was grasping for these girls to answer the deep needs inside of me, I found my desires only increased and became more desperate.

As I began to walk with God in college, I knew that I needed out.

So I began praying for God to break me from these desires. Despite all my external changes, the desire remained. Although I resisted and searched more for God, I still wanted *the* beautiful girl, wanted to possess her wholly, make her mine. It appeared my prayers weren't enough.

After months and months of wrestling with so much shame and guilt, I didn't know what else to do, so I began praying that God would take my desire for beauty away. I thought that if I could just get rid of my desire for beautiful women, then I could finally be right with God. I prayed he would help me bury and kill this desire. As I prayed for this, I remember thinking — *Great. Now God is going to send me an ugly woman because of this. A woman who loves God, but looks like a duck.* So you can imagine that praying to God like this began to scare me, but I was that desperate. But it didn't seem to be working. God didn't take this desire out of my heart, no matter how hard I prayed about it. Every day it was there, again and again, as I walked to class and sat in my room.

So I grew to have a love/hate relationship with this desire for beauty. Secretly in my heart I wanted it, but I also felt so ashamed and guilty for having it and what I had done to try to satisfy my desire. Before long, I was convinced beauty was the devil's creation to draw me away from God. If I could just kick this thing, I thought, I would be flung into the arms of God as a saint, and become a perfect son.

———

But instead of sainthood, all I received was more heartache, temptation, and struggle. I really had no idea what to do about it. God wouldn't take this desire away, so I stopped asking him about it. I did my best to control and manage it. For years I felt like I was shackled to it and that my desire for beauty would forever be a barrier between myself and God, and so I left it out of our conversations.

One weekend I was home in Nashville having lunch with a pastor friend named Scott. Although I don't remember how we got on that exact subject, he seemed to have a different take on the whole beauty issue. He told me "beauty is *good, true,* and *of the soul.*"

This confused me, because my conclusion was that beauty was *"bad, false,* and *of the Devil."* God and beauty seemed like contradictions to me.

I asked, "Are you telling me that beauty was *not* created by evil as some kind of temptation to keep us from God?"

"No," Scott responded, "God created it, not the Devil. In fact, God created beauty to draw us to *him.* We can see his finger-prints in the sunset, in a painting, and throughout creation. He poured beauty into creation to make us yearn for the Artist. Why do you think you are even looking for beauty in the first place? It is because you were made in his image. God is a lover of real beauty more than you are."

God a lover of beauty? Now, this was an unusual thought. I wondered if God was a butt man, or more of a legs guy. Is that what Scott meant? I wasn't all that sure.

So I shared some of my history with him. "Look where my search for beauty has taken me — how can that possibly be of God?"

He explained: "Beauty is meant to take us on a search, like we do when we look for a beautiful painting or picture, or read a great book — or even, oddly enough, see a pretty girl. But the beauty of this world is only an appetizer in our search for a greater meal than it can provide. The beauty we see on earth can only give us a taste for what is to come. It is only a shadow of the Author of the beauty.

"Our problem is how we place it on a pedestal as our object of worship instead of letting it take us into the deeper search for what and who created it. How many people marvel at a painting, and then start talking to it? Who marvels at the brush-strokes and colors, and praises the canvas about it? Do people read a book, look at the cover, and start talking to the book telling it how great and insightful it is?"

I laughed. "They'd be crazy."

"Yeah, we would lock them up in a mental institution.

"The painting draws you to *the painter* and the words on a page to *the author*. Beauty was created for us to seek to understand *the Creator*. Think for a moment about all the verses in Scripture about the mountains, creation, and God. That's because he is the Designer. They reflect his brilliance, and we think about his greatness when we see them. But is that what most guys do with a woman's beauty? Most guys try to grab it, then throw themselves down to worship it, and make *her* into their god."

He then got personal: "Xan, you are trying to find the perfection of beauty in something where it can never be found. You've missed the point. Beauty was never meant to be worshiped the way you do. I think you need to pray and ask God to give you new eyes to see where real beauty can be found, not the air-brushed fantasies of magazines, supermodels, and pinups. It's not that you desire beauty too much; it's that you've settled for so little. Your hopes of it are placed in the wrong thing. What if there was more beauty out there than you have ever known, but you just didn't have the eyes to see it?"

I left his office rattled. I went to a park down the road to think through what he'd told me. Sitting down in the grass beneath a tree, I wrote and wrote in my journal, and prayed about what he had said.

I knew he was right about how I had made feminine beauty my god. I had looked for it to fulfill something that seemed impossible to fulfill, and I had used it to try to validate myself, bring me pleasure, and satisfy my every fantasy. I had used beauty to get acceptance from my friends, and I had judged my worth by how much of it I had or didn't have in my life.

Sitting right there in that park, I asked Jesus to forgive me for how I had made beauty my idol and my god, and how I had used images and girls rather than him to answer my desires and longings to be noticed and accepted. And then I asked him something I had never asked before. Instead of asking him to take me away from beauty, I asked him to take me deeper into it—to help me see *real* beauty and understand it. Both in him, and in a woman.

It felt almost sinful to say this. I had never heard a church sermon or anything in the church talking about my longing for beauty and these desires, but I prayed anyway. I prayed that this pastor Scott was right, and somehow there was an answer to these desires that had to do with God, and that there existed a fulfillment of them in him. I prayed for him to show me the fullness of the beauty and for him to give me new eyes so that I could see it.

Then I started to wonder if God would really answer me, or if Scott was just crazy.

One day, I found myself flipping through this enormous art book of paintings and sculptures when I came across a series of paintings of naked women—but these were not the naked women that I had gazed upon in secret in magazines or on my computer screen. These pictures did not in the slightest way arouse me. I could look at them with the same reaction I would have had if it had been a piece of fruit or a rock instead. These women were not tanned and skinny; they were pale women with very rounded bodies. As I flipped through the pages of the book, I would see a sunset by the sea that took my breath away, and then I would turn the page to one of these ghostly-white women lying nude on a couch, and it would almost frighten me.

But as I read through the descriptions of the paintings, I realized the painter was trying to capture what I had been longing for all those years before: the beauty of a woman. The text below one said that at the time it was painted, this was what people admired, drooled over, and idealized in a woman.

I laughed.

White as porcelain? Overweight? Are you kidding? This is beauty?

But the description went on to say that years ago, a large, voluptuous body was a prize. White skin was considered beautiful because it meant the women did not have to work outside in the fields or on the farm. A thin body was looked down upon, because it represented being underfed, poor, and in the working class. Large women were admired because they had money, could afford to eat, and had time to just lie around on couches all day. The slinky, tanned girls on the covers of today's beauty magazines would have been unattractive in that day, and unimpressive to most men of the time. They would have passed them over for the beauty of white-skinned, large women like the ones in these paintings.

As I looked through that book, I couldn't believe it. It was the complete opposite of today's image of beauty. If this was true of their beauty back then, it meant that our definition of a woman's beauty is merely a cultural thing. It was a view I had been sold by advertisers, marketers, magazines, and Hollywood. It was only an opinion, and not a truth, nor a standard I should expect. It was hard to believe, but apparently my picture and definition of beauty was completely shaped by the world and culture around me.

After thumbing through this book, wondering if Scott was right and God had made my desire for beauty, I felt that I had no idea what that real beauty was. It seemed part of the matrix of my world, and evil had shaped it into a certain version for its own purposes. I found that I was completely blind to what beauty really was.

I must confess, usually the last place I end up looking for answers is Scripture. I seem to look everywhere else, and then after there is no other place to turn, I ask God and he shows me. Well, I had done this again in my search for beauty.

I was hoping for some biblical idea of beauty, which up until a few months before I didn't even think existed. I still wasn't even sure if it would be there. But the pastor was right again. God and his people were speaking and talking about beauty throughout the Bible.

David prayed, "One thing I ask of the LORD, this is what I seek: that I may dwell in the house of the LORD all the days of my life, to gaze upon the beauty of the LORD and to seek him in his temple."[1] And another psalmist wrote, "Strength and beauty are in his sanctuary."[2] Hmmm . . . *to gaze upon the beauty of the Lord?* Beauty had to be more than the way he looked. The more I read, the more I began thinking Scott was right about God being the Author of beauty. He seemed to be the crown of it—the source of it. This also meant beauty was more than a tall, skinny, tanned figure with a round butt. I recalled a verse that said, "The god of this age [Satan] has blinded the minds of unbelievers, so they cannot see the light of the gospel of the glory of Christ, who is the image of God."[3]

The word *blinded* really stood out to me here. I wondered if this was what had been done with beauty. Through the art book, I had seen that the beauty I had been seeking was defined by the world, and here this verse was saying that the "god of this world" was determining the way we saw things to "blind" us to the things of God. Had we been "blinded" to true beauty in this same way?

It took me back to evil and deception and how it is always offering a copy of the thing my heart truly desired. What if my desire for beauty was for something God had created? If it wasn't going away, was there something that could fulfill the ache? Just as deception had made counterfeit answers to lead me down the wrong paths, what if God had an answer to my longing for beauty? What if the reason I had never explored more is because I could not even see there was more to it? Had my eyes been blinded to the real version?

This made me think of a vacation I had been on a few years back.

———

I spent a week in Hawaii with my dad, mom, and brother. It was incredible. We spent most of our time—except for meals and sleeping—in the middle of paradise on a white beach. It was the place to be. The sky and ocean were cast in vivid blues. The water was as clear as a crystal, and all the palm trees swayed to a light breeze. We were simply amazed with all the beauty before us. We didn't want to be anywhere else; we were right in the middle of paradise.

But each day, we looked out near the edge of the shore at the end of the beach and saw people snorkeling. From the surface, it looked as if they were gazing upon a white sea floor and a few black rocks. It seemed such a waste with so much beauty around us, why go below? Why not just taste and enjoy what was before us? Why go deeper? But as people kept walking over, putting on masks, and going below, curiosity finally got the better of us, so, on the last day, we decided to go snorkeling.

We rented some equipment and went over to the rocks. I was expecting to see the same thing below that I had seen from the surface: clear water, white sand, and rocks. But once

I'd squeezed the mask onto my face and dropped my head into the water, I was in awe.

This was beauty.

I don't think I have ever seen so many colors in one place. There was an entire world of fish of every shape and color just inches from my face. The rocks and coral sparkled and danced as the waves played with the sunlight streaming into the water. These hues were bright and vibrant; some I couldn't remember ever seeing in nature before. There were bright purples, oranges, reds, and yellows that radiated. We were stunned. So this was why people were going below! There was so much more beauty down here—from the surface, we would never have guessed it existed.

When we finally returned to the beach, I looked at the people bathing in the sun—one of whom I had been all those days before—and laughed. I was just there ten minutes ago, and had missed out all that time. Until I was willing to venture deeper, I would have never discovered more. I was so content to settle with the limited palette of a few colors above the water, when just below the surface there was an entire rainbow of them on display. All I had to do was put a mask on and go below the surface to see it. I was content with the limited view of beauty, when there was so much more if I was willing to keep searching for it.

In the same way I had thought the beauty I was beholding was all there was to see while sitting on the white sand beach, I had confused beauty with only being about physical attraction. Maybe every woman, in her own way, is beautiful and desirable? Maybe it was something much deeper? But I had never considered there was a deeper and more enjoyable beauty to seek and gaze upon somewhere else, and in something deeper. It seems most of us sit on the beach staring, content with what is on the surface. Most of my life I had settled for that too. But what if just below the surface—in the "inner" world—there was more? Could there be more to what I desire, more to what all that longing was for a woman?

Although I was being called to turn from this sin in my life, it appeared that God wasn't calling me to give up beauty; he wanted me to go beyond the surface and understand the heart of my desire for it, and in continuing my search, I was about to learn some glorious discoveries about this desire.

the heart of a woman

There are three things that amaze me —
no, four things that I don't understand:
how an eagle glides through the sky,
how a snake slithers on a rock,
how a ship navigates the ocean,
how a man loves a woman.

PROVERBS 30:18-19, NLT

I was in a bookstore a few years ago, alone and cruising through
the history and religion sections. While skimming over biog-
raphies of presidents, sports stars, and war heroes, one book
cover jumped out at me and caught my attention. I froze. I
recognized the woman's face on the cover almost instantly,
though I did not recognize her name. It took me a few seconds
to place how I knew her, and then it all came rushing back. It

was a woman I had seen naked on the Internet.

Staring at the cover, I realized this was her biography — the story about her life. I hesitated to touch it. "Do I really want to know about her life?" Before that day, I knew nothing about her other than that she was some type of porn star. I had never needed more information — not her hometown, what she liked to eat, or her hobbies — her naked body was all I had ever wanted from her. Out of curiosity, I chose to pick it up, but only after I was sure no one was looking. I found a corner of the bookstore away from people and started to read about her life.

I'll admit it was a bit weird.

I was surprised at her story; she began as a cute, normal, little girl. She played and laughed and did all the stuff little girls do. But only pages into it, her life took some tragic turns. She'd had some really bad breaks. For one, her father had left her mother early in her life. And then, after her mother remarried, her stepfather sexually abused her while she slept. It got even worse. At ten, she was raped by an older boy in the neighborhood. Remembering those moments, she asked herself, "Was this [sex] the 'one thing' boys wanted?"

These events shattered her life. She wrote, "I was afraid of my own shadow, I felt hollow inside . . . gutted . . . and raw . . . left with nothing but an empty carcass to carry me. I wished I were someone else. I hated myself. . . . How could I deny it? I was a whore. And I was only ten years old."[1]

I sat there in shock as a few tears trickled down my face. A ten-year-old girl who saw herself as a whore? I felt so sorry for her. She had been a normal little girl who had been robbed, used, abused, and tossed aside by men all her life. I felt no lust as I read her story. Whatever I felt while looking online at her naked body was completely shattered. I had nothing but compassion for this girl who never had a chance from the beginning. Men had used her and stripped her of her true beauty, her heart, and her purity before she was even a teenager. But what made this so personal for me was not just those men and their horrible acts, but that I was one of them.

By logging on to those sites and buying those magazines, I had only continued to rape and steal from this woman's soul as well as that of many others. I did it alone and in the dark, but I had used her in the same way as these men of her past. She was an object to bring me pleasure. I had used her with no thought about who she was as a woman or that she was even a real woman with a story and a past. I thought about her question, "Was this the 'one thing' guys wanted?" Looking at my life, I realized why her response was, "Yes."

As I have already mentioned, I was never very close to girls growing up. Most came at me from a distance, like Lindsay Lane in the school lunchroom. Girls were a mystery for me. I just never got close enough to girls to become friends with them. Plus I didn't really care about their friendship as much as wanting their beauty and their bodies.

My excuse for not having female friends is they were very awkward and intimidating. They weren't like guys, where you could keep the conversation on sports or coming over on the weekend to play video games. They wanted to talk about feelings and relationships. They required you to understand them and the things they liked. Talking to girls required me fighting past fears of rejection and fears that I might not know what to say. You had to know how to talk about girl stuff and ask girl questions. I didn't have a clue what to say to a girl or how to say it. Who was I supposed to practice on? Or learn about this from? There weren't classes on it, and I didn't have a sister.

It was a long process, but I think it was around my senior year at the University of Tennessee when I really started to wake up to the idea that there was more to a woman than just her looks, and that there was something deeper inside of her that my heart really wanted to know.

I finally met a girl who I connected with as a friend. Initially, I wanted to date her, but God had more for me to learn from her as a friend than I knew. She reminded me of a supermodel. She was tall, dark skinned, had long, flowing hair and a smile that knocked you off your feet. She was the kind of girl that you could find on television turning over prices on a game show.

The typical reaction of the guys who met her was either drooling or shock. It was only after a few minutes of talking to her that they were instantly wrapped up in her beauty and eager to ask her out. It seemed she caught everyone's eye. She had the star quarterback at Tennessee calling, and at least a dozen frat boys on her trail, and me, the undercover guy who was her friend.

But something odd happened. We actually became friends. Not best friends, but good friends. We connected as people, rather than as hunter and prey. As I listened instead of lusted, I learned that although a Christian, she had a somewhat troubled past. Despite being beautiful, she carried a lot of pain with her from all she had been through. But when you looked at her, you didn't see any of that. In fact, nobody knew. Everything on the outside said she was a beautiful, charming, and a perfect Christian girl. No one saw the damage, struggles, and pain she carried in her heart. They didn't care much about that—they weren't interested in getting any deeper. She was a Christian, and she was super hot—that seemed enough for most guys.

Guys would ask her out, and after about two dates, they would fall in love. They would start calling regularly and do incredible things to win another date, but—because of her hurts—the more they fell for her, the more she ran from them. Guy after guy would come, fall for her and her beauty and her charm, and then she would push them away, time and time again.

It was worse because, being beautiful *and* Christian, she was just the type of girl every guy would love to marry. Great, upstanding guys with the best of intentions would pursue her, but she always turned them away. It wasn't long before she got a "runaway bride" type of reputation. No one could figure it out. Was she just a cruel heartbreaker? Why did she run from these great guys who were charming, moral, strong, good-looking, and stable?

Because of her, I had to rethink my interactions with girls. I started to see what was happening. This girl was not perfect, and she was sick of guys who couldn't see that, because they never looked past the surface of her green eyes. On the inside, she was really just like everyone else. She had insecurities about her body, fears about relationships, and struggles with things every person does. She once told me, "Guys settle so easily just for what is on the outside, as if they don't really care what's inside. They don't even know how to ask me about the real me. How can they like me, when they don't even really know me yet?"

Through our conversations, I heard in her voice a desire to be noticed, and seen, but not just as some idealized beauty pageant contestant. She wanted desperately for someone to know her—really know her—and not just be fascinated by her appearance. She wanted someone who would pursue her heart. Someone who would ask questions about deeper things than what her major was and what she liked to do on weekends. She wanted someone who could understand she had issues and problems as well, and would be willing to help her work them through. I think her fear was that these guys, who were so taken by her external beauty, once they found out the other side, would not be so excited to hear about all the troubles in her life. She wanted to be loved for all of who she was, the good and the bad, the ugly and the broken. I realized that most guys just couldn't believe this stunning woman could have any deep broken parts or that there might be some ugliness on the inside of her.

And so, she kept turning them away. Again and again.

And no one could figure out why.

I found out an interesting statistic the other day. Did you know there are around ten million girls who have an eating disorder in the United States? Doesn't that seem unusual to you? Anorexia and bulimia are diseases that most men can't comprehend. To eat too much food and throw it up, or to eat none at all and starve yourself? Why would anyone ever do that? But although it's strange to us, and is kept secret by most women who have an eating disorder, the addiction is similar to the struggles men have with pornography.

Statistics say that around half of the women in the United States will have an eating disorder for at least some period in their lifetimes. And 80 percent of women are dissatisfied with their appearance. Ever notice all those diet pills and workout video commercials on television? There is always a new diet coming out and fads to trim weight and get the figure you want — and almost all are directed at women.

Why do women worry so much about how they look? Why are girls flocking to get cosmetic surgery, buying the latest fashions, painting their faces with makeup, and reading all those beauty magazines?

John Eldredge, a Christian counselor and author, wrote in his book *Wild at Heart* that "every woman is asking the question, 'Am I beautiful? Am I lovely? Do you notice me?'" As I thought about the statistics of eating disorders, it made some sense. I wondered if part of the problem is that our society tells women we don't want their hearts; we only want their bodies and faces and legs to be beautiful. Even the porn star wrote in her book, "I longed to matter to someone, to feel loved and needed . . . I was . . . willing to sacrifice my body to bandage my soul."[2]

It reminded me of a night in Knoxville a few years back. I was at a place called Cotton-Eyed Joe's with three of my friends. It is a country bar with a dance floor the size of a football field. I'd left my friends to go to the bathroom, and made the long trek to other side. As I looked to my left, there were seven girls dancing on a bar. As I looked to their right, I saw what had to be around twenty or thirty guys just staring at them. I stopped and watched. And although I would have usually joined the guys looking at the girls, this time I watched the guys. I looked at their eyes, which were glazed over, almost trancelike, and transfixed on the girls. They weren't moving. They looked like statues far off in some fantasy world. And then I looked at the girls, and how much they were enjoying the attention of it.

They weren't offended; they were loving it.

Looking back, and thinking that if those girls were asking the question, "Am I beautiful?" then it made sense. Those girls wanted to feel beautiful, lovely, and to be noticed. And yet, to them, this might be the only way someone would ever see anything in them. They were willing to stand on a bar, wear next to nothing, and flaunt their bodies for these men, just to be noticed and adored for a handful of minutes.

I thought about evil, and how it is always offering us a cheapened, forged version of the thing we really desire. I wondered if God had put a desire in a woman to be beautiful, be seen, and feel lovely, then evil was right there, showing a girl a false way to satisfy that yearning. I wondered if that is what was happening in the bar, with eating disorders, all the crazy diets, and wearing those tight clothes. Was it a desire of their heart and of the soul to find a beauty that would be admired? I wondered if girls had the same problem of believing there is anything beautiful inside them as well? Maybe the matrix of the world never lets a girl believe there is anything below the surface that is lovely and beautiful either?

As I thought about all of this, I thought back to that girl I had seen online and had read about in her biography. I thought maybe it was partly our fault, that we had never seen women for more than pretty faces and sexy bodies. We had told them "this is beauty" and this is what we wanted, and they were puking, starving, going under the knife for it, and wearing next to nothing. What if the world around them had told them they needed to be perfect on the outside — and so they were doing what was required of them to be "all" that, no matter the cost?

Again her question echoed in my mind: "Is this the 'one

thing' guys want?" Maybe every girl thinks, *Is this the only way I can be seen, noticed, and maybe someday loved?*

———

As I continued to discover more about women's hearts, I remember watching a commercial with a girl in a shower. She was putting shampoo in her hair and making noises. At first, it had me lusting, but then I started thinking about what I was lusting over. I realized she was moaning and having an orgasm over the soap in her hair. I had watched things like this all my life and lusted, but now as I watched, I realized she wasn't an object, she was a real person—a girl with a heart and a soul who probably lives somewhere in L.A. I imagined she was trying to make it in acting and took this call by her agent about a shampoo commercial to pay rent. And so she went down to audition for the "shampoo commercial."

There was probably some corporate man in New York who had worked for the shampoo company who had made a call to a talent agency and said he wanted a hot chick with long legs who could moan in ecstasy in response to his shampoo. And she had to be good enough at it that men in America would lust after her, and women in America would want to buy it so they could be her and get men to lust after them just as they were after her—because of shampoo.

I bet that when the guy in New York had to decide which girl to pick, he didn't care about anything but her legs, her butt, and how she could moan. I imagine during the tryouts the line of questioning wasn't, "Tell us a little about yourself, why you're here and what you want to do with your life." I bet it was lining up the girls like *American Idol* and seeing who looked the best moaning. I bet he didn't care what she had to say, or that she had a real soul, or that she was anything more than just a body. He really didn't care about anything other than if it was going to make him enough money to buy a sweeter car and live in a sweeter place that would impress his friends and maybe get him a hot chick too.

It was a new one for me. I saw this "sex object" as a real woman. And I was pretty ticked off. A girl was being used and exploited because people actually bought things sold by hot girls. She was stripped of who she was, how she was created, and was worth no more than moaning over soap.

I kept finding it all around—in commercials, on billboards, and in magazines. Women's bodies dangled out like pieces of meat, and then a quick flash of a car tire or a beer. But the part that got me really ticked is that for over twenty years of my life, it had worked. I had bought into it. I had listened to that New York man in that corporate office about what beauty is, and he had triggered my desires for it like I was a trained monkey so that he could sell me something. And I had bought into these lies that a woman is nothing more than a hot body, a sculpted face, and moaning.

I knew in my heart, there was more to beauty, and more to what I wanted than just a hot body, or the satisfaction of watching a girl dance, or looking at her naked on the Internet. I did want more. But it was just very hard to understand what that desire was really for, considering how much of a mess I had made of it and how "good" evil was at deceiving me.

I wanted to find out God's version, but most talks I heard in church and the books I was reading were more concerned with telling me to stop lusting, stop dating, or to put a filter on my computer so I would stop viewing the wrong sites on the

Internet. Looking back, I think it would have been much more helpful to teach me to understand the thing I really wanted or how I could find it, along with those things. I don't want to be super critical, but no one was talking about that or what this desire was in us that took us into those places.

They just said "no."

God's help in showing me the heart of a woman was not through books or sermons, but by blessing me with a friendship with a new girl named Lindsay—not Lindsay Lane. God sent me a friend—a friend who was a girl. And this time, instead of trying to date her, I became a friend. A real friend. We met while working together after college with Young Life in Knoxville. I think she was the first girl whose heart I ever got to know as purely friends. We laughed at the same jokes, made up skits for Young Life, and had fun with each other. We just seemed to connect. Plus, we could have a deep, sincere conversation about God together. I got along better with her than any girl I had ever met before.

I think Lindsay was the first girl I noticed for who she was and not just what she looked like. From our time hanging out, I knew Lindsay wasn't perfect, and she knew I wasn't either. It was one of the first times I really opened up to a woman and saw life through a woman's eyes. I learned more about women from her than I could from any book or any dating relationship. With Lindsay, I was completely myself. And more than that, I was learning how to speak, engage, and be present with a real woman and her heart, and it was great.

I think that's the first time I found beauty, but it was different. It was not airbrushed or perfect. It was real, but not the kind you could touch. It was a girl being vulnerable. It was a girl who had a passion for Jesus and for serving others. And loving people where they were. She was also broken and had struggles, and yet she did not let those hold her back from experiencing life. Author Francis Schaeffer calls people "glorious ruins," because we have both glory and a broken nature. And for the first time, I saw glimpses of that in a girl—and it was beautiful.

I began to learn about women from a woman. I got to hear directly from her mouth about some of a woman's desires and experience her tenderness. I asked her lots of questions, and she invited me into her longings for what she wanted in a husband. She told me her list of what she wanted in a man: a man who would respect her, guard her, value her heart as much as her body, and see the real her and her beauty from her inside out. I knew this in theory and from books and my other female friend's frustration, but I had never heard it from a woman's mouth before. It was beautiful—more beautiful than I had ever expected. And yet, something told me, this was still only a mere taste.

I realized that what I had always wanted with a girl was what Adam and Eve had, but lost: to be naked together and unashamed. In high school and into college, I had always tried to do that physically. I tried to fulfill my desires for beauty and intimacy with fantasies and pornography, and with girls in a bedroom, but I always came up emptier after dabbling in them. What I really wanted was a girl I could bare my soul to, who I could let my heart stand naked before and she wouldn't laugh or walk away in disgust. This was what I had truly been longing for all those years without realizing it. It was part of

God's design for a husband and wife. I still wanted to meet a girl I was physically attracted to, and there was most definitely still the sexual stuff, but there was also something beautiful I found in our friendship, something deep, rich, and connected to my longing. There was even beauty in her brokenness and struggles and pain as she brought it to her God, and spoke to me about it.

Lindsay was the first girl who offered me hope and made me want to go out, find, honor, and serve a girl who I could one day call my wife.

It was during my friendship with Lindsay that I watched Mel Gibson's *The Passion of the Christ*. The obvious point of the film was to experience Jesus' crucifixion and suffering, but what stood out nearly as much to me was the scene in the movie of Jesus with Mary when she was about to be stoned to death. Mary the prostitute—the whore who had given herself and her body to the men of the town. Adultery was her job, but Jesus approaches while the men are ready to stone her for her actions as the law of Moses required.

When asked what he thought should be done with her, Jesus draws the line in the sand, and says, "Whoever is without sin, cast the first stone."[3] In the movie, you see all the men drop their stones and walk away.

The whole movie had me emotional, but I cried as I watched that. It was such a powerful moment for me. Jesus went against what every other man had done to her. He showed her compassion and love, not exploitation or condemnation. Jesus knew she was guilty, but he spoke in her defense, and saved her life.

He saw something more than just a whore, and he stepped in to defend her for it. We don't know the details, but that moment changed Mary.

I thought about the porn star, those girls dancing on the bar, and that girl moaning over soap. They all were there and doing those things probably because of men — men and their superficial impression of what beauty was and how it could be used to get something, whether that be money, sex, pleasure, or fame. I just wondered what our world would be like if instead of using women for their beauty, we served women instead. What if we protected and guarded and actually listened to and learned about women, instead of trying to take advantage of their beauty in one way or another? What if, instead of staring in wide-eyed wonder at a girl in tight clothes, we actually saw her the way Jesus did? I admit, this is not easy.

I began to realize this was actually what God had planned in the first place — for a man to guard a woman's purity instead of plunder it. And although I had gotten some really screwed up messages, and interpreted them in the wrong way, the church was just trying to teach me this exact point — my job was to guard a woman and the beauty of her heart, because one day that heart was to be for her husband to spend the rest of his life discovering and enjoying.

I started having flashbacks of all the girls I had ever talked with, dated, or had as a friend. How many had I defended? How many did I look to guard and protect, and show them there was more to them than the world was telling them? How many had I used? How many girls had I really thought of beyond their looks and their bodies or to meet my immediate needs?

For the first time in my life, I wanted to change. God was changing me. There was something in me that really wanted to honor, guard, defend, and draw forth beauty, and not use it for my own instant urges. I realized God had set up these boundaries so that I could actually partake in this deep discovery and enjoy it through marriage. I must admit, I have not been perfect in this, and I have made lots of mistakes. But in the process, I have learned to receive grace, and let it lead me into truth. The truth that I really do want to be a man who looks at a woman and can see what she is like on the inside. And it's happening. Jesus is healing me.

To skip ahead, I am married now. I won't even pretend that I fully understand the essence of a woman's heart or have gotten close to the deepest parts of my wife's heart. That's only beginning. But I am learning much. There is so much more to women and our relationships with them than I ever imagined. God continues to open my eyes, each day, to more of what my desire for my wife, Jayne, is really all about. And I am realizing it is worth the wait. And regardless of where we've taken this desire, he is a God willing to open our eyes, change our hearts, cleanse us, and bring us into the real thing.

strength

They were brave warriors, ready for battle and able to handle the shield and spear. Their faces were the faces of lions, and they were as swift as gazelles in the mountains.

1 CHRONICLES 12:8

It all started as a routine day of school at Franklin Road Academy. There was the usual morning hallway chatter and updates, while my homework from the previous night remained just a blank sheet, crumpled somewhere in my bag. My second-period art class would disrupt it all, as I sat on a stool lost in a world of art and imagination. My friend Jeremy approached laughing. He had a challenger for me in an arm-wrestling match. But it wasn't a guy who I had been challenged to arm wrestle—it was a girl.

As the promoter of the event, Jeremy took only minutes to broadcast it throughout the hallways and into every classroom. I loved getting attention, but this was not the kind I wanted. Not only that, but I was scared. I had always been a small guy, and in eighth grade I didn't weigh all that much either. I was already questioning my strength as it was—I didn't have any room to lose ground, especially to a girl. And this was some girl. She had arms muscular enough to throw my manhood into a tailspin.

Needless to say, I had no desire to arm wrestle her. I was convinced I would lose. I kept putting it off, thinking that after a few days, like most things at that age, people would forget. But this is the kind of thing guys love to see, and my floundering had only increased the drama of it all. So I finally agreed to the match. It might have been only two people there, but in my mind the entire school circled around us like it was a playground fight.

I gave it everything I had. I mean I poured every ounce of myself into that moment. I grunted, pushed until the lactic acid burned, and pressed my muscles to their limit. Before I knew it, it was over. To everyone's surprise—even my own—I'd won.

The crowd faded away, and there I was—alone. There was no shouting or bragging or slapping me on the back because beating a girl was really no proof of anything. Even though I had technically won, I had lost. I had been singled out among all the guys as the weakest, the smallest, and the least likely to beat a girl. It was in that moment when I first realized I lacked the thing that really seemed to make a man—strength.

———

I knew as a kid that a man was something far different from a woman. It didn't take angels to come out of the sky and announce it. From Popeye and his bulging muscles, to Tom Cruise in *Top Gun*, to Donnie in high school, the signs were everywhere.

These guys had the masculinity a boy needed. To me, their strength seemed about as important as finding food to eat and air to breathe. From kickball at seven, to parties on the weekends in high school, to dating a girl, these all required me having it. I knew that a man was supposed to be tough, strong, dominant, independent, powerful, and courageous, just like these guys—and if they were a little reckless and unpredictable in the process, so much the better.

I can recall as a little boy, wanting to be around things that displayed such raw power. Big things, dangerous things, things like bulldozers, guns, trucks, chainsaws, power tools, and fireworks. So I burnt things, crushed things, and blew them up.

I can remember experiencing strength at scout camp when building a fire and watching it blaze for hours. It was a fire I had created with my own hands, a few matches, and sticks. I also remember rappelling off a hundred-foot tower, and then later that day firing a .22 rifle at the range. I loved it. Weapons and bullets and targets to put holes in. I couldn't believe they would trust me with a gun or jumping off a tower or starting a fire. I was pretty impressed that I didn't kill anyone—or myself.

However, that was an unusual experience. Usually the message was something a bit different. I remember coming home from that trip so excited, and in response being told by my mom I was not allowed to have a gun. It was too much, too powerful, and too dangerous for me to handle as a young man, she'd explained. She had her reasons, but I got the impression that the world was a dangerous place—too dangerous, in fact—and that I was incapable of handling it. As proof they always regularly showed me newspaper clippings about boys dying in car wrecks, or injuries from accidents with lawn mowers, or guns going off at the wrong time and wounding someone.

From what I heard I figured that whatever this craving was, and whatever these desires were to be strong and fight guys, have fireworks wars, or jump off cliffs—they were definitely not spiritual ones. The idea of a guy finding strength or displaying strength, and this being somehow connected to God or Jesus, was almost a joke to me.

I got the impression a guy needed to let go of all these desires, so he could find love and peace and sit in the arms of Jesus. Jesus did not want me to find courage or strength or fight—it seemed he wanted me to be more soft and sensitive and tame. He wanted me to sit and read and sing more. The offer of Christianity did not seem to speak to this growing desire in me to find and display strength. Although they kept calling the gospel the "good news," that news was not very good for a guy, especially for a guy who got laughed at in an arm-wrestling competition with a girl. There wasn't much hope I could redeem myself or find redemption in Jesus. It seemed if anything, they were asking me to give up my search for strength.

In seventh and eighth grade I had signed up for football in hopes to find my strength. I did not play because I was good or promising, or even because I knew how to throw a tackle; I just needed to prove something to myself and to those around me. I needed to feel strength inside me. I had to show there was something powerful, dangerous, and violent in me if provoked, and football seemed the best place to bring it out. Before long I was hitting, sweating, straining my muscles to new limits, and even bleeding. It felt like real man stuff every time I put on the pads and the helmet, tackled someone or got tackled, and left practice beat up, sweaty, bruised.

But after a few weeks, my dream started to sink. Because of

my size, I found football to be more guts than glory. No matter how much I poured my heart out on the field, I just didn't have what it took to knock down any of our bigger players. Most guys on the team had some real weight to throw into a tackle. The weight I was carrying was not so much mass and muscle as it was helmet and pads. No matter how well I followed the fundamentals of sticking my shoulder into a guy and wrapping my arms around him, the best chance of me actually tackling a running back twice my size was to throw my body at him and just hope he would trip.

Near the beginning of practices, we were assigned tackling partners of similar height and weight. Ironically, my best friend Sam was chosen as my tackling partner, probably because we were the smallest two guys on the team. By about halfway through the preseason practices, the tackling drills were taking their toll on both of us. I think it was obvious we would not last another season, but we wanted to impress the other guys and the coaches, and quitting the team would have only made us look like wimps. So we came up with a plan. Each time during tackling drills, when one of us lunged to tackle the other, the guy waiting to be tackled would throw himself to the ground as if he had been hit by a truck.

It was a brilliant plan, and we soon had become the models of form tackling for the entire team. I learned a lesson in football that I would carry with me for years: if I couldn't find my strength, then I would just fake it.

I entered high school small, and though I grew taller, I never got much bigger. My chest was flat, and my arms were almost nonexistent. I remember one girl I was dying to date told a friend of mine, "I might date him if he was bigger."

Bigger? Stronger? More powerful? Ugh. As if I didn't feel frail enough already.

The theme continued throughout high school, though, and I realized I needed a new plan. So, my junior year, the same year I bought my Jeep, I decided to do something about it. I went into a sporting goods store and bought a weight-and-muscle-building program in a box. As soon as I got home, I opened the package, watched an instructional video, studied the workout chart, took the supplements, and hit the gym like I was Arnold Schwarzenegger heading for Muscle Beach.

It took only a few months before I started to show some improvements. I was bulking up a bit and putting on real muscle. The program was actually working—my chest grew, and my arms began to bulge as I kept lifting. It felt incredible. And for the first time in my life, I had a taste of what it felt like to look strong. It was real muscle. I could feel it and see it fill in my shirt.

I could tell people around me started to notice, and girls started talking. I remember returning to school after a summer of long workouts. When I pulled up in my Jeep wearing a "wife-beater" to see a friend named Michelle, I could tell in her eyes that she had noticed. She touched one of my arms and with passion in her eyes said, "Wow."

So I worked out more and more. And the more I grew, the more I wanted to grow even larger and impress more girls. Before long I was buying muscle magazines, eating weight-gainer powder for snacks, looking up to muscle heads, and doing exercises like "donkey squats."

The gym was unlike anywhere I had been before. These

guys loved their bodies and wore tank tops and spandex most of the time to show them off. Many of them went to the tanning salon daily. They were big dudes, with some serious strength. They stacked forty-five-pound metal plates on bars and then benched them like they were plastic. I looked at my new heroes with envy.

I sweated and grunted beside them from high school and into college. But after a few years, I started to notice the oddest thing: insecurities. It was as if I could look inside them and watch as they pounded those plates up and down. It appeared as if they weren't straining against the weights as much as against their own fears, doubts, and questions about their strength. It was as if many of them had the same questions and maybe struggled with questions about their strength as men, as well.

In the midst of this testosterone, bulk, and grunting, I realized my plan wasn't going to work. While putting on more muscle got me some looks, it wasn't going to bring what I really wanted. I began to see that I was working out for the same reasons these guys were working out. We thought we could change how we felt on the inside by changing what we looked like on the outside. We wanted to feel and be strong, but all we could do was look like it. It wasn't working. We were hollow men.

To be honest, I continued to carry these questions with me for years, on into college. After working out for around four years straight, one day I just gave it up, put down the weights, and canceled my gym membership. It wasn't that I had found the answer, I just knew it couldn't be found at the gym.

The change wasn't until years later, when I attended a

Christian conference where a professor named Dan Allender spoke. He is the president of Mars Hill graduate school in Seattle. At this conference, he spoke about how we were designed by God in his image back in the Garden of Eden. During his talk, he read it right from the book of Genesis:

> Then God said, "Let us make man in our image, in our likeness, and let them rule over the fish of the sea and the birds of the air, over the livestock, over all the earth, and over all the creatures that move along the ground."
>   So God created man in his own image, in the image of God he created him; male and female he created them.[1]

He explained that when God made Adam and Eve, he made one as a male in his image, another as a female in his image. Each was created to reflect the heart of God—his traits and personality—like we were little versions of him. But he said that since God does not have a body, it was reflected in our souls, hearts, and desires. He then read verses from Psalms:

> One thing God has spoken,
>   two things have I heard:
> that you, O God, are strong,
>   and that you, O Lord, are loving.[2]

Dan said these two characteristics of God—strength and lovingness—are how we most reflect God and his image. He explained how this word, *loving*, also had a meaning of mercy and tenderness. He said that a man is to reflect more of God's strength, and a woman is made to reflect more of God's tender lovingness and mercy, but we both have strength and love within us.

He said God created women with more of a nurturing spirit, and thus she has the womb, births and nurtures the baby, and tends to be more affectionate, compassionate, and relational. He then explained how a man was more broad shouldered and physically stronger, because he is to carry the burdens and protect the family. God made Adam the head of his wife, Eve, showing his responsibility. Dan said God created all these physical and emotional things to show the deeper reality about the soul within each of us.

It was like the clouds parted as he spoke. All those years of trying to find my strength in sports, girls, guns, and working out started to make sense. There was something in my design that was crying out and trying to find its place. God had designed me with the desire to be strong, and I had been struggling to uncover that strength all my life. This desire was not something unspiritual or ungodly. It was incredibly spiritual, and that was the whole reason I was looking for it. This was good news. But there was still much more to learn.

I read more about it in some books. In them, I discovered that our generation is mostly blind to true gender issues. Guys today don't have a clue about what it means to be a man, made in God's image or how that might be different from how he made a woman. No one is talking about it.

People discuss gender roles, but they squash and bury the truth that there is indeed something very different between a man and a woman.

———

I was reading a few statistics about guys the other day. Did you know:

- Men commit 90 percent of major crimes.
- Men commit 95 percent of burglaries.
- Men commit 91 percent of offenses against the family.
- Of drunk drivers, 94 percent are men[3]

Why is it that men are so much more violent than women? What in us provokes this kind of anger and need to strike out and harm others — often women? Why so much self-destructive behavior and violence in men?

I wondered if it was evil playing off our God-created desires again. If I looked at my life, I was constantly looking to other things to give me the feeling of being strong. I was faking it, and doing all kinds of things to feel like a man. But never once did I consider it to come from God. Could there be a matrix of counterfeit strengths set to deceive us and keep us from what God really wants us to find as we pursue being strong? Could all this violence be about a man trying to feel strong?

The statistics reminded me of fifth grade when I learned how to cuss. There was something powerful in these words, even the ones I didn't understand. The reactions they brought to some people's faces did something for me. Most ten-year-old kids were afraid of these words. They were hesitant and afraid to speak them (probably a good thing looking back). But they did something for me, and made me feel something inside that words like "nice" and "cool" and "awesome" could not.

I took cussing to a new level that year. I spoke the words with confidence and courage like I had invented them. I could use them creatively as a subject, verb, or adjective at will. And often, I used them together completing entire sentences with nothing but them. I remember one day thinking to myself, *I cuss a lot.* And I didn't know why.

As I thought about this, I realized that almost all of these statistics, and even my cussing, had to do with power. Psychologists tell us that crimes such as rape and sexual abuse are not about sex, but to prove the man's power—or strength—over women in general. It's about domination and control. I wondered if all of these acts of violence were really examples of guys falling for a counterfeit way to find strength. "Strength gone bad," so to speak. As if evil was right there, willing to give a man a false sense of strength through these ways of anger and violence, even cussing.

Dan, that professor I heard speak, also said something else that blew me away. He said that it is a man's desire to feel strong that takes him into pornography. I thought he was crazy, because I had always seen it just as lust and nothing more, but he said that pornography is usually about the desire and need to feel powerful over women. The guy makes love to the woman in his mind and feels like a hero. Dan said, "Most pornography is about violating a woman's beauty. When a man masturbates to a picture, he uses it to feel something inside that is missing and wants to be strong." He was right. There is a power and sense of strength when a man has sex with a woman, whether in his mind or in a bed. She can become an object he can control. He gains a sense of power. I wondered if rape was just the next level from pornography? Again, it was evil's answer to giving men a false answer to the true desire.

Living in true strength was God's intent, but pornography, triple-X movies, and "picking up chicks" are all perversions of it. Instead of showing strength in a man, evil offers a false version and saps it away. The promise is it gives him a feeling of strength, but always leaves him feeling weaker and emptier than he was before. I'd done that. Even my desire to date had not been about the girl as much as how strong I would look with her hanging on my arm. It was as if evil was whispering, "Feel strong. Feel powerful. You can find it here, and now. God is holding out on you, and with me you can have it all."

This shed new light on these statistics about violence and the problems with pornography, because I was part of it. I was angry that I didn't feel like a man, so I played football, worked out, cussed, tried to act tough, and fantasized about women. Looking back, I was searching for the strength God had put within me to find. I had gone just about everywhere else to look for strength, feel it, or gain it, except God. I had accepted the false again and again because I had no idea there was a true form or where I could find it. Up till that point, I didn't know he even cared.

In the Bible, there is a lot of war imagery. "Fight the good fight."[4] "Endure hardship with us like a good soldier of Christ Jesus."[5] The description of the armor of God found in Ephesians. Strength is needed to fight our spiritual and worldly battles.

Look at the men of the Old Testament. There were many warriors. They were serving under the banner of God and for his purpose. I think that is the big difference. When we think about our strength, I think we need to consider, is our strength used for good, for God, and under the banner of love, or do we use it for evil and for selfish reasons?

Many people use strength to impress people and look good,

but God had something far different in mind when he made a man. Man was definitely to defend, and to bear burdens and stand firm, and to be patient. But a man was also meant to fight for what is right. The Bible says, "Hate evil, love good."[6] I don't know about you, but if I hate something, I feel some aggression. Could that aggression be meant to be used for good and against evil?

But here's another thought about this whole strength thing. What if we were made to fight — not against others, but against evil? Against the powers of this world, and against injustice? Paul says, "For our struggle is not against flesh and blood, but against the rulers, against the authorities, against the powers of this dark world and against the spiritual forces of evil in the heavenly realms."[7]

My next questions became, "What does it look like to find my strength and use it for God? What does it look like to offer my body and my soul and wield strength for his purpose?" I knew it wasn't by getting drunk and picking fights or just sitting around or waving a stick and casting out demons in the sky. Again, I found no greater source to really understand this other than the Bible, and finding examples of men who walked with God and had discovered their purpose in strength. I discovered that God was actually showing himself through these men. And in fact, his strength coming through men was his primary way of letting people know about himself. Read what the great warrior David had to say about strength:

You armed me with strength for battle;
    you made my adversaries bow at my feet.[8]

In your strength I can crush an army;
with my God I can scale any wall.[9]

He renews my strength.
He guides me along right paths,
    bringing honor to his name.[10]

The God of Israel gives power and strength to his people.[11]

Now from the book of Hebrews:

Gideon, Barak, Samson, Jephthah, David, Samuel and
the prophets, who through faith conquered kingdoms,
administered justice, and gained what was promised;
who shut the mouths of lions, quenched the fury of the
flames, and escaped the edge of the sword; whose weakness was turned to strength; and who became powerful
in battle and routed foreign armies.[12]

Men who were powerful in battle? Strong? Courageous?
Fearless? All the things I had wanted as a boy to become.

According to this, God seemed to be in the business of
bringing a man into true strength—from weakness to strength
through him. And more than anything, it had nothing to do
with showing off, or appearing strong, or using it to hook up
with girls, or having personal power over people and things.
In fact, usually when God showed up, the people doubted the
man it came through. It was all through faith, and trust, in the
name of love, and belief in the power of the kingdom of God.

I really believe I will spend my whole life trying to find and offer strength. I really believe it is wired into my design by God. There are really only two options for me: to find it on my own through some false version or feeling, or to find it in God and use it for good.

So how do I walk in this strength in Christ? How do I offer this to others and the world? What strength do I have that is unique to me, and how will God use me? What weakness is in me into which God can bring his strength? Where will God use me if I walk in this strength? And for what specific purpose?

These are some of the questions I am asking now and am still trying to understand. I wish I could write more, and I wish I could fill these pages up with wonderful stories and explanations, but this is where I am right now. I am still in the middle or even at the beginning of discovering what real strength is, and how to live in it.

In fact, just a few days ago my friend Cory, during a time when a few of us were praying together, said to me, "I need you, Xan. I feel like you are only willing to offer about 10 percent of yourself to others, and you hold the rest in. But we need you. There is more in you we need to become what God has called *us* to be."

I was shocked. I had never been told anything like that before. My strength is needed? And I might be offering only 10 percent to others?

What if it is true of all of us? What if we embraced a true version of strength? Could *our* strength under Jesus be needed in the world? Is that what is missing today? Real men walking in strength and through love? Even Jesus said, "Love the Lord your God with all your heart and with all your soul *and with all your strength* and with all your mind."[13]

I am starting to really believe that is true. I believe I have offered some strength, but I haven't really reached out into what I can offer. I think I am afraid of it, scared of what others might think. I have to be reminded that it doesn't rest on my abilities, but on God's. I know that I want to offer more. And I don't want to spend my life faking it—I want God to awaken me to real strength. And I want to offer that strength to others, and to use it for good.

the role

The Lord has assigned to each his task.

1 CORINTHIANS 3:5

After finding Jesus on that river, and feeling him work in my life in a fresh and real way, it was very natural for me to get fired up about sharing him with others. I remembered him saying, "The harvest is plentiful but the workers are few."[1] Well, I wanted to be one of those workers and be used for his kingdom.

Over the years, I had picked up a few things from other speaking evangelists who had shared Jesus with me from a stage. It was sort of the basics of sharing the gospel—what you might call Evangelism 101. First, you told lots of stories about how crazy and wild you were before you'd found Jesus. If possible, stories that involved drugs, fame, women, parties, sex, and guns.

Second, you tell all these stories in the past tense. Your audience needed to know that sin was behind you and that you have walked away from it. You are done with the old life and its problems and are now fired up for Jesus.

And third—and possibly the most essential for evangelism—was you have the people close their eyes and raise their hands to accept Jesus as their Lord and Savior at the end of your talk.

I figured I was the perfect candidate for the job. From my time in the frat, I had lots of stories—wild, crazy, radical stories—so I figured I would put them to work and start raising hands for Jesus.

My first chance came at a college meeting where I was asked to give my testimony. Weeks before the meeting, I started scribbling on paper all the things I had done. I had notes on stories about women, parties, and drinking. I spent hours thinking about my lists of sins and how I could weave them into my testimony. I figured the more, the better. I gave my talk, and about 90 percent of what I shared was about how crazy and rebellious I was. I was half-proud of them because it made me look like a real wild, tough guy like all those other guys who had preached at me when I was growing up.

In the last part of my talk, I tried to copy those other speakers by telling the people how Jesus had turned my life around and that my struggles were now gone and I was riding the waves of hope, peace, and love propelled by Jesus—and they should too. Then I asked all the people to close their eyes and examine their lives and raise their hands if they wanted Jesus in it.

Hands shot up all over the place. I had them pray this four-line prayer I had memorized the night before, and afterward, it was all over. The crowds left. People got Jesus. I had been used by God. It was powerful. But what felt even better was that they received him because of *me*. *I* had convinced them with my testimony. Xan the Evangelist. My talk was good—really good. With my crazy stories, and making my conversion to Jesus sound real dramatic, the emotional appeal had drawn them in. And then after that people started coming up to me on campus who couldn't believe my stories and my changed life and wanted to hear more.

Over the next few years, I got hundreds of people to raise their hands. I was getting so good that near the end of it all, I expected at least one-quarter of the people to raise their hands anytime I spoke. The feeling that came with people raising their hands and receiving Jesus was incredible. To be used by God? It was better than making a tackle, catching a pass, or even scoring the winning touchdown in a game. I was doing God's work—work that brought people into eternity.

I was convinced I could become the next Billy Graham. I could just see the stadiums packed with people wanting to hear my stories and raise their hands. I was convinced I was God's number one extreme crazy-story hand-raiser, and I was ready to take my testimony to the world.

In the midst of all this, I was given an opportunity that I had been waiting on for a long time: My entire fraternity had come to hear me speak. A friend had stood up in our chapter meeting and told the guys they should all come support me. So they did. Almost all of them were there. This was my real heart, to get my fraternity saved—to tell them about Jesus and have them all raise their hands.

I had a packed audience of around two hundred and fifty people, seventy of which were my fraternity brothers. My other talks went so well, I didn't change anything except to add a few more fraternity stories. I started with all these wild things I had done in the fraternity, having sex, getting drunk, and cussing left and right. I talked about how all those other things didn't fulfill, and how happy I was now with the truth of God, his Word, and his Son, Jesus Christ. And then I told how Jesus grabbed me, saved me, and how I was not sinning anymore because of it—not drinking, partying, or struggling with all those temptations. Jesus was all I needed.

As I came to the end, I had everyone close their eyes. I looked around the room and asked anyone who wanted this to raise their hands. A few hands went up, but as I looked to my fraternity's section, none of them had raised their hands. Not one.

I didn't understand. Why not? As I went home that night I was troubled. Didn't they see their sin? Didn't they want Jesus? Hadn't they seen how different I was? Didn't they hear my story? But I wasn't going to give up. I knew God wanted to save them. A few weeks later at a Bible study led by my friend Rick, I was convinced that guys would start coming to something in the frat house. But no one came. I couldn't believe it. None of them wanted their life changed? No one wanted to stop lusting, cussing, and drinking beer, and finally find the true answer to their desires?

I couldn't figure it out.

I knew these guys were hurting and lost. I had heard their stories in the Smoky Mountains on our pledge retreat. I knew they were struggling. I knew they needed Jesus. I could see it in their faces and hear it in their words. I knew it because these guys had been my best friends, and I had sinned with them.

So I did a little "outreach" work to try to get them to the

study. I would knock on their doors five minutes before the study and remind them. Yet still none of them came. They all just hung out in their rooms watching television, playing video games, sipping beer, or talking while we waited, sitting in a circle of mostly empty chairs with our Bibles.

But hope returned one night after the study when a guy named Ray grabbed me in the hall and asked if we could go to lunch and talk. I agreed.

I was very energized about this. I knew he wanted it. This was it. He had heard my talk and had thought it over, and wanted to ask Jesus into his life. I just knew it. This was big. He was strong, confident, and a man people followed in the frat house. Can you imagine a top frat guy converting to Jesus? How many others would follow his lead?

So we met. After eating a sandwich, and a bit of chatter, he looked me in the eyes and asked, "Do you struggle, Xan? I mean, with your faith? In believing all of this stuff about God and Jesus that you preach about? Do you still have questions about God? Questions about why you are here, and if this is really true? Are you that confident in what you're saying?"

This was not what I was expecting. Still shocked, I asked him, "Why are you asking?"

He explained, "It seems like every Christian is trying to sell something. Sell Jesus like he is some great product. They use all these big words, and talk about how great this part and that part is, and how they are doing so much better than they were before, and not hurting or struggling and are so happy."

He kept going, "It's not that I have a hard time believing Jesus and his words—I guess I have a hard time believing someone like you and what you are saying. You seem more like a salesman selling a product."

I just sat there. Speechless. Shocked. I knew he was saying something true, but I didn't want to admit it. What was I to tell him? I didn't know what to do. I didn't want to tell him I still dealt with some of those things. I couldn't admit it. I was too afraid after all my great words and testimony about Jesus and me being a Christian—and things being so great—he would see me as a fool.

But apparently, he already did.

I spent a few weeks thinking about Ray's comments. And although I did not want to see it, I realized what I had become—the person Jesus was always frustrated at—a Pharisee. I was a religious man who walked around with a big head and thought too highly of himself to admit his needs and his brokenness and struggles to others—or even to himself.

And here is what Jesus said of such men:

> "Everything they do is done for men to see: . . . they love the place of honor at banquets and the most important seats; . . . they love to be greeted in the marketplaces. . . .
>
> "You are like whitewashed tombs, which look beautiful on the outside but on the inside are full of dead men's bones and everything unclean. In the same way, on the outside you appear to people as righteous but on the inside you are full of hypocrisy and wickedness."[2]

This was me. I was all looks. I had just put on another mask. I had switched from Party Xan to Christian Xan, but hadn't changed much of what was inside. I wanted to bring people to Jesus, and I thought I had good intentions. But I was trying to sell people Jesus in order to receive the validation that came from them believing and accepting my words and raising their hands, like a car salesman closing a deal. It wasn't really about Jesus or the cross, as much as it was about getting them to like me and look up to me so that I felt I was doing great work for God.

I wanted to earn people's approval by being in the spotlight, having a great testimony and sharing it. With all those people raising their hands, I felt like I was doing something great. I realized I had exalted myself—not Jesus or God or anything other than me. I was convinced, if I'd been honest, if I'd gotten on that stage and said, "I believe all this, and I am walking with Jesus, and God is bringing me new hope, but I still struggle with temptation and doubt and sin and am working through it," people would throw me off the stage. Who would look up to me then? After all, that's not what all those Christian extreme people did when they got up, right? They were solid. Convinced. Sold out. Fired up. Didn't question things, or struggle—or so I thought.

I thought back to those fraternity guys, and how none of them raised their hands at my talk. I wondered if they could see right through me, and if that was why they were no longer my friends. Maybe that's why no one called me up to hang out anymore, and why no one showed up at the Bible study. And why they had nicknamed me and a few friends "the God Squad." It wasn't a compliment. I was an untrustworthy salesman.

I wondered if, in my efforts to be a witness and trying to be a light, if I had separated myself from them, and not the other way around. I realized all I had been doing was telling them I was better than they were through my "nice and clean Christian testimony." Maybe they couldn't relate to me or even see the light of Jesus inside through the self-righteousness on the outside.

I soon realized that I had gotten it wrong and missed something. They weren't about to come to our fraternity Bible study to listen to more of me speaking on a soapbox. I wondered if my evangelism wasn't all it was cracked up to be. Was it really more about me trying to convince them than it had ever been about Jesus and the Holy Spirit changing their hearts?

———

God brought me to the Scriptures and the story of Moses. It was around the year 1446 BC when Moses was wandering the dry, arid wilderness. He had escaped Egypt and spent the last forty years in the desert. He was an outcast and alone. It seemed a leading role for Moses in God's kingdom was far from a possibility.

Then one day he came across a burning bush while attending a flock of sheep. The Lord spoke to Moses. He told him he had heard the prayers of his people who were under heavy bondage in Egypt. God told Moses that he would be the one to lead the millions from slavery and into the wide-open Promised Land flowing with milk and honey.

It was the role of a lifetime for any hand-raising evangelist. He was to be God's voice — his quarterback, team captain, and number one man. Talk about power, authority, and respect! What an honor, right? Moses should have been stoked. But listen to Moses' response to God:

"Who am I, that I should go to Pharaoh and bring the Israelites out of Egypt?" . . .

"Suppose I go to the Israelites and say to them, 'The God of your fathers has sent me to you,' and they ask me, 'What is his name?' Then what shall I tell them?" . . .

"What if they do not believe me or listen to me and say, 'The LORD did not appear to you'?" . . .

"O Lord, I have never been eloquent, neither in the past nor since you have spoken to your servant. I am slow of speech and tongue." . . .

"O Lord, please send someone else to do it."[3]

God's people are enslaved, persecuted, and dying at the hands of an oppressive nation. God comes to Moses with the offer of a lifetime, but Moses doesn't jump. He is saying, "Me? Yeah, right! Don't you know my weaknesses? My insecurities? My fears? Why not send someone else? Someone more qualified, more prepared. I can't be the guy for the job. You must have made a mistake."

Maybe Moses' fears were, at the heart of things, my fears as well. Although I really thought I was preaching God's true message at the time, maybe my arrogance came from a deeper insecurity inside me. Considering where I was in my faith—I did still have questions and many struggles. Looking back, I think I was afraid to share that, and so I really just tried to imitate others. I spoke what I thought I needed to say and how other extreme people talked about Jesus, so I didn't have to share myself. What I realized is I had left out my true self. The "me" that God wanted to use. I was just like Moses; although I was out speaking, inside of me, I never thought God could really use me, my story, and all my weaknesses.

Because of it, I had become all hype and hypocrisy.

I still had plenty of temptations and failings, but I hid them. Instead of letting others see my frailties, I kept them private. I would smile at my fraternity brothers and "look saintly" and cuss at a car driving by. I would put my Bible in my front seat, so others would see it, but rarely read it there. I never shared the struggles and questions and the needs I still had; I hid them. Up on stage, everything was good; my life was great, Jesus was great, but behind closed doors, although I had answered a lot of questions and struggles, I still had a lot more of them to answer.

I realized that day at lunch, Ray had seen right through me and called me on it.

I soon came to see the disciples Jesus chose were not as radical and celebrity status and perfect as I used to think. His followers were normal guys: fishermen, a tax collector, a blind guy, a man with a bum leg, mental cases, broken people, and lots and lots of losers. You would think he would have gone after the strong, powerful, and influential, but Christ passed them over. He seemed to go after the low-income, rough, and uneducated. He went after the guys who could never get it straight. He was constantly correcting them, and they were constantly screwing up. They were a mess. They were nothing close to perfect. Some were claiming power, others were using violence, and others didn't even get who Jesus really was, even though they had followed him for years.

I felt relieved.

Then I read something from a book by Mike Yaconelli that summed it all up:

Look at the Bible. The biblical writers did not edit out the flaws of its heroes. Like Noah, for example. . . . Noah was courageous, a man of great faith and strong will. . . . Noah built a huge ark in the middle of the desert because God told him it was going to rain. No one believed him, but the rains did come and the flood happened, and after the water receded, Noah triumphantly left the boat, got drunk, and got naked.

What? *Drunk and naked?* I don't recall any of my Bible teachers or pastors talking about Noah's . . . uh . . . moment of indiscretion . . . er . . . weakness . . . um . . . failure . . . very few ever refer to Noah's losing battle with wine.

Why should I be surprised? Turns out *all* of the biblical characters were a complex mix of strengths and weaknesses. David, Abraham, Lot, Saul, Solomon, Rahab, and Sarah were God-loving, courageous, brilliant, fearless, loyal, passionate, committed holy men and women who were also murderers, adulterers, and manic depressives.[4]

This was encouraging to know, because although we all have weaknesses and strengths, God is appointing us for his work anyway. God is not looking for our perfection, but our willingness to step out in faith through Jesus. Not one of them was without sin, or without flaws, or struggles, but that wasn't what God cared about when appointing his leaders. He wanted men of character and integrity, and that came out of their willingness to serve him, to keep following, trusting, entering into his words and his promises through faith. Listen to what Paul says:

I came to you in weakness and fear, and with much trembling. My message and my preaching were not with wise and persuasive words, but with a demonstration of the Spirit's power, so that your faith might not rest on men's wisdom, but on God's power.[5]

He goes on to say in 2 Corinthians 12:7-9:

Satan's angel did his best to get me down; what he in fact did was push me to my knees. No danger then of walking around high and mighty! At first I didn't think of it as a gift, and begged God to remove it. Three times I did that, and then he told me,

> My grace is enough; it's all you need.
> My strength comes into its own in your weakness.[6]

I had heard these verses before, but they had new meaning. They gave me permission to not have things completely figured out and together. My life has often been very performance-based with lots of striving, but this showed me the gospel wasn't meant to rest on my power or my performance, but in Christ's work and his grace. He is enough. It appeared, yet again, that the gospel was Christ's strength moving in on man's weakness when submitted to God. And yet, somehow, that was the exact thing I wasn't giving over—my weakness. God's power wasn't just when I was acting right, it was available to me during my trials, and my struggles, and during temptations. I never talked about finding God in those places.

Guys like Ray didn't care if I was perfect—in fact, trying to be perfect was what scared them off. They wanted to know I was real. They didn't want to know how to be perfect, but how to handle the struggles they faced daily. I hadn't realized that this was exactly what the fraternity was waiting to hear from me — they were waiting for me to be honest.

———

Ray and I met again. And what had started with my awkward and forced attempts to convert him turned into a time, once a week, of great conversation. I got to sit down with him, this crazy guy, who was willing to be honest about his crazy life, if he just had someone who would be honest back. And Ray didn't hold back. I remember him saying, "I love hooking up with girls, and I love Miller Lite beer," among other things. He would wake up on a Monday at 8 a.m. — hungover or at a girl's apartment where he'd spent the night — and drive to the frat house to meet me for breakfast. Regardless of where he had been the night before, or what he had done, he would be there waiting for me — ready to talk and hear my questions, as well as ask me a few himself.

He wanted to share his life. He wanted to talk about his questions, family, and God. As we talked, he would also ask me personal questions, and I would have to open up about my hiding under the religious mask, and trying to be perfect. But then he would listen to what I was learning about God, and I would really get to share with him my hope in Jesus.

Many times we would sit and sit for hours and even miss class, because we were so caught up in the conversation. We would talk about God a lot, sometimes open the Bible, some- times pray, but everything we talked about was real and spiri- tual. It was simple and about life, about struggles, and what we both really wanted out of life.

I wondered if this was true of the other guys in the frat house too, or was Ray the only one who wanted this? Did others have questions and have no one to share them with? I wondered if even my words up on that stage had only repelled them from ever talking to me about them. Did they see me as a religious freak who thought he was perfect and had nothing in common with them?

So I did something that was a bit controversial. I started going to parties at the frat house again. I would station myself around the kegs of beer and the dancing, and would just hang out and talk to people.

At first, it was very awkward. Everyone looked at me like I was crazy, and I got a lot of those "What-is-he-doing-here?" looks and "Aren't-you-one-of-those-religious-people?" stares. But the more I was there, the fewer I got. Guys started to see me as one of them again, and even came up to talk when they saw me.

I was there, not to judge them, but to love them. I would often pray before I left for the party and ask Jesus to bring conversations and people and protection. I am not saying it was easy, and there was plenty of temptation to slip back into what I had been my first few years at the frat, but God really did give me strength in those times. He had prepared me to go back.

It was amazing the things that would happen. A guy would stumble over to me, drunk, and say, "Hey, we should hang out some time. I would like to talk." And then he would stumble back over to the dance floor, and back to the girl he was grinding with. But the next day or so, I would find him and ask him to breakfast, and we would talk. Or a guy would be filling a pitcher of beer at the bar and stop to talk to me. What I found was guys really wanted to talk and share. They really needed someone to open up with who wasn't going to give them quick religious answers or judge them. They needed someone who had been in their shoes and understood them and was willing to listen.

I kept going and having more conversations at those parties. There were some nights where I spent three hours at the bar talking with guys about true and deep things right in the midst of the party. It was amazing, because we were in the middle of a place that seemed to have so little to do with God.

I remember one night sitting at a bar with a guy named Brad who did not know Jesus. We were looking out at all the people dancing. He turned to me and said, "I have been doing this for seven years of my life." He pointed to all the people and spoke again: "See all these people who are laughing and dancing and acting like this is the time of their lives? They're not happy. This doesn't work."

I just nodded. I asked him a few questions about it, and before long, we were in a great conversation about life in the middle of that crowded party.

Although many did not know it, they were searching — searching in the middle of alcohol, parties, and drugs — for God. Not all of them wanted me there or wanted to talk, but many of them did. And instead of preaching, I was there on a barstool ready to listen and finally share my search, my longings, and my desires with them.

My senior year of college, I realized how unique my situation was. I had the trust and respect of many of the hundred or so fraternity guys. I was an insider. I was one of them. I had gone through pledging, been next to them puking in the toilet and during hell week. I was not a master theologian or counselor, but they would listen to me because I was like them. I talked, dressed, and acted like them, except with Jesus in me.

No one else was able to talk with these guys in this way. They wouldn't listen to religious preachers, but many would let me ask them questions and even listen to me. Why? It was because my stories were part of their stories. If I was willing to share with them my own, it was a doorway to see their life and their story. Their story was not something on a Hallmark greeting card, but neither was mine. I realized my role wasn't to preach fire at them, or to save them, but to help them understand their lives by sharing myself, and being me. They didn't want fake stuff or a "testimony." They wanted to hear the raw stuff. The real stuff.

And I also understood their longings and their questions for beauty and strength and brotherhood, and hiding behind a mask, because I was in the middle of discovering it too. And yet, I was different, because I knew where answers could be found. I knew their lifestyle wasn't the answer to what they were searching for, but instead of standing on a soapbox and telling them, I often waited for them to ask. I gave them the freedom and permission to be who they were. Instead of expecting something from them, I built friendships, and through those friendships helped some of them interpret their pain, their hiding, and their struggles.

I earned the right to be heard.

Instead of expecting them to come to the Bible study, or hearing me talk, I went to them. I went out to the parties, their houses, and the places where they were. Sometimes I went because I wanted to; other times I went because I felt God calling me there. Then one day, it hit me. This was it. This was true evangelism and sharing of my testimony that God had really called me to in this moment in time. It was not by standing behind a podium and telling people how to fix their lives and be like me — but being with them, among them, loving them, and showing them I was just like them. I was a young man searching and exploring and looking everywhere to find life, and had, much to even my own initial objections, stumbled upon the Source.

I think that was the moment when I realized I was to show the love of Jesus and give my testimony, through both the joy and the heartache, and in my weakness and my questions as well as in the answers I had found, and not just through raising hands. My testimony and my life were not to be about my performance, or a happy and perfect made-up life. It was a story about how God had come for me, and was still coming for me, even when I had turned away and run.

I am beginning to believe my life, just like every life, is very unique. It is my own. I don't have to pretend to be someone else, or fit into someone else's testimony. I have a story about God. A story that isn't a nicely packaged testimony, but a real one — a story that speaks about Jesus and his work in me.

And I hope it is a story worth telling — not because it makes me into a hero, but it proves the love and faithfulness of God.

wrestling men

This left Jacob all alone in the camp, and a man came and wrestled with him until dawn.

GENESIS 32:24, NLT

About two years ago, before I moved to Colorado permanently, I visited Colorado Springs for a retreat and also to have coffee with a man I greatly respect. He is forty-something, a counselor and an author. We had hung out a few times before this and talked about ministry and life, and he had asked me a lot of questions. These were all very personal, deep questions, which took me some real soul-searching to answer. I wanted to be honest, but inside there was also a fear his questions might reveal something I didn't really want to find out about myself, especially in his presence. I also desperately wanted him to like me and to call me again sometime to hang out.

Although I wanted that, I didn't want to be obvious about it. It just felt too awkward to tell him how much I'd enjoyed hanging out with him, appreciated all the questions he'd asked, and that I hoped we would do it again sometime. However, I thought if I impressed him with my words and my confidence, he might want to keep hanging out with me.

It was during our conversations, as we sat in a Starbucks, right in the middle of a passionate sentence of a speech aimed at wowing and impressing him with my insights, he interrupted me.

"I think there is a boy inside of you."

This definitely caught me off-guard. No one had said anything like this to me before, especially right in the middle of a speech meant to impress. I had no response. I just sat there in silence.

His eyes just stared into mine, waiting. It was one of the scariest moments of my life. What do you do when a man calls you a *boy*? I wondered if I heard him wrong. It took me a moment, but with a somewhat shaky voice, I asked, "What do you mean by that?"

"Xan, I think there is a boy inside that you hide from. He is a part that you show no one. I think much of who you are is still that boy trying to hide. You need to ask Jesus to come for that boy. If I were you, I would go out today to the Garden of the Gods Park and ask Jesus to come for you."

Within minutes he was gone, and I was left alone in Starbucks with the weight of his words. I clung to my cup of coffee with both hands. I felt rejected and hurt. I had stepped into an older man's world—a man of great insight and wisdom, and he had shot me down. I had opened up to him, and as a result, I felt like he had reached in, grabbed my heart, and crushed it. He had seen something inside of me, something young and immature and childish. He'd seen right past my big words and bravado, and he called me a boy.

I was pissed. I mean really, really pissed at this guy.

Yet I found myself pulling into the Garden of the Gods Park less than a half hour later, just as he said. I got out, slammed my car door, and paced furiously in a section of the park where no one was around.

Instead of some nice little prayer and my heart being poured out before God, I hurled stones across the valley floor and kicked up red dust, cursing this guy and his nerve. I then raged at God for letting a man representing him make such a statement to me. I mean, how dare he? Who did he think he was anyway?! He didn't really know me.

Why had I opened my heart to this guy? I must have been crazy! Why had I allowed him to say those things? What did he really know about me? I mean, I was twenty-five years old—I certainly wasn't a boy anymore. I was a grown man.

"I *am* a man," I repeated to myself. "I *am* a man. *I am a man.*" I repeated it over and over as I wandered through the park, hoping it might sink in.

Two days and a flight later, I was back in Knoxville. As I stepped off the plane, I decided to deny that conversation had ever happened. *Forget him*, I thought to myself. And with that, I locked what he'd said away and didn't tell a soul. I decided I would go on with my life, like nothing had ever happened.

———

Roughly two years after this, when that conversation was all but dead and gone, I went to a cabin in the woods with some friends. We had been going through a book together and decided to take a guys' weekend to go four-wheeling, eat pizza, and play cards. It was early in the morning on Saturday, and we were lounging around eating cereal, laughing, and watching television when the show *American Chopper* came on.

The show is about a bike shop where custom-made motorcycles are built. The show is really a circus — the whole thing could be a Jerry Springer episode. There is yelling, laughing, and random fights that break out between the two brothers and the father who own the shop. We all sat transfixed as they drilled holes, cut steel, and welded metal to create a custom motorcycle.

None of us were mechanics, and I don't usually watch shows like that, but the grit, dirt, and raw testosterone thrown back and forth between father and son, brother and brother, mesmerized me. I looked at all the guys around me on this L-shaped couch, and almost laughed. We were like kids sitting there drooling over candy or something.

The show was hypnotic. Something about watching this family of men turn an old bike and a pile of scrap metal into a work of art with a blow torch and workshop of tools spoke to something deep inside each of us. None of us talked. We all just stared into the television.

As I left that day, I had to ask: What was it about that show that caught our attention? I didn't think it was the bike, because none of us had a bike. I wondered if there was more to it.

———

For a long time, it appeared the way to manhood was by being crazier, stupider, wilder, or more outrageous than my friends. Sam, Eric, Matt, Brad, Paul, and David were my proving ground during high school and against whom my manhood was either won or lost.

By college, it was a new group of guys to impress—my fraternity brothers. When they picked me and invited me into their frat house, they initiated me into their brotherhood and showed me the ropes. Then they laid down the gauntlet: They were wilder, drunker, crazier, and tougher than my high school buddies had been, and so now I had to prove myself again at a whole new level. Here in order to win, you had to take more girls back to your room, show more attitude, and drink more beer.

After being initiated and becoming a brother, I watched the same process happen year after year. Young, confused freshman faces—not unlike my own—would walk into the house, go through rush, take a bid, and then look to the older guys to tell them what to do and be. I still remember those fresh faces coming to us and trying to earn our approval and respect. Each year a group of new guys would come in and do it all over again. Year after year. The freshmen were looking to us for answers. But thinking back, I am not sure if the guys they looked up to had any more of an idea on how to live than they did. We had initiated each other almost like a gang that tried to learn bravery, courage, and family from each other without any good examples of men around to show us.

The problem was that the thing that had been missing most in our pursuits to become men was just that—men. There were none around. Even when I joined a college ministry, it was all student led. It was as if all my life I had been learning to be a man—not from men—but from other *boys*. And since I was never taught, led, and grown into the things of life by a community of men, I never saw a need for men, or had any desire to learn from them. If it had been offered, I would have rejected it to go hang out with guys my age. I was confident that I could find it on my own and blaze my own trail.

Or at least I had thought I could.

———

This man's words—"there is a boy inside of you"—continued to eat at me despite trying to shake it. So I did some research. Okay, call me a geek, but it was something I felt I needed to find out about. I read some books about being a man, and I discovered that we are living in a time like none before. We live in an age where men, in general, are missing.

Up to about one hundred years ago—before the industrial revolution and the invention of factories, cars, and transportation systems—men worked at home or in very close proximity, so they were available to their families much of the day. Grandfathers and uncles and cousins usually lived close by and shared their lives together. Up until about a hundred years ago men and boys were always together.

Because of this proximity and the few schools, children often learned their occupations from their fathers or a close relative. The father usually trained the son for his career in an apprenticeship system. They lived and worked together learning through trial and error, spending time on the job with the boys always at the feet of these older, wiser, and stronger men, working the family business—whether it was cutting down trees or welding metal or running the general store. And when the father got too old, the oldest son took over the business and stepped into his father's shoes. He'd learned everything he needed to know about life and work virtually in his father's shadow, so he could handle it. Remember, Jesus was a carpenter. His father taught him the trade.

Now, this might sound a bit archaic, and the last thing some of us want to do today is follow in our father's profession, but part of the reason we feel this way is that we are so disconnected from our dads. It may be obvious, but when men worked closer to home, there was simply less distance between them and their families, both physically and spiritually. Boys learned to be men by spending most of their time in the shadows of men, and just part of the time hanging with their friends and testing each other's strengths and courage. In that day, it was being with men that gave meaning to this play, not the play that defined being a man.

I realized this doesn't happen anymore. Men work miles from home and are gone for long hours. Divorce has risen, and many guys don't even live with their fathers. Sons don't spend nearly as much time with their fathers, and fewer and fewer sons seem to follow in their father's footsteps in the family business. Most guys are raised by moms or by nannies — and most teachers in schools are women.

Men are missing.

As I rolled this around in my mind, I realized my father was around when I was a boy, but I had pushed him aside or never saw any real need for him. Hanging out with my dad just wasn't that cool. Instead, I hung out with guys around my age, and if I ever wanted to talk about something, I had gone to my friends, not my father, my grandfather, an uncle, or some older man. I'd never considered that I might actually need the counsel or guidance of older men. As a teenager, I was sure I didn't need anyone but my friends. What did older guys know anyway? They were of another generation, out of touch, and had lived in another time, another world. So I pushed them aside, always looking instead to my friends.

I thought back to that *American Chopper* show. I wondered if we had watched not because of the tools, engines, and motorbikes, but because we were fascinated to watch two brothers work side by side with their dad doing something they all loved. I wondered if there was some buried desire and need in us that we longed for and didn't even know. Something that those guys were getting on that show as father and sons working next to each other, laughing, sweating, and screwing up together, sharing the journey. I wondered if in some way we were all boys, still needing men to show us the way.

I thought back to that conversation at Starbucks—could that man have actually been right?

If I am honest, this man in Colorado Springs had awakened me to something I did not want to deal with. In the weeks and months following, I couldn't keep his words out of my head. I kept feeling a young place in me that I resented and hated. It was part of why I was so insecure and afraid of other guys. I still felt like a boy, and I didn't know what to do with that place in my heart that needed help. I had grown in many ways, but as I grew, the boy inside stayed a boy. What was I supposed to do with that boy in me? Where was I to go with it? Who was I to share that with?

One morning I was reading some Scripture and came across a story in the Bible about a man named Jacob that I had read before.

Jacob was out in the evening on a journey when someone approached him. It was God. And with no reason or explanation given as to why, it says they started to wrestle. They wrestled and wrestled all that night and into the morning hours. Jacob would not let go. In fact, Jacob had such a tight hold that God had to injure him before he would let go. But still Jacob said, "I will not let you go unless you bless me."

God asked him, "What is your name?"

"Jacob," he answered.

Then God said, "Your name will no longer be Jacob, but Israel, because you have struggled with God and with men and have overcome." The story ends with Jacob walking away with a limp and a new name because he had wrestled with God.[1]

The story seemed a bit absurd to me at first. But after thinking about it awhile, I wondered if this was sort of a metaphor for becoming a man. We all need to rub shoulders, get dirty, and wrestle with someone stronger than us to learn what it takes to prevail in this world. Jacob wrestled with God and asked for a blessing. But God didn't just bless him, God gave him a destiny: to be the father of a nation of people who would be called Israel after him.

I thought back to when I was a kid and when my brother and I would wrestle with my dad on the living-room floor. We would sneak up to try to catch him by surprise so that we could bring him down to the floor where we could get our arms around him. His stubbly face would brush against our smooth skin as we strained our muscles against his, and we'd scrap with him until every ounce of energy was drained from our bodies. It was a test of strength, boy versus man—and I realized now how important that was.

I wondered if that was how I was to become a man—a series of metaphorical wrestling matches against stronger opponents until I met God face to face on my journey. It was like every struggle of life was really a wrestling match—whether it was finding a career, talking about my purpose and direction, what different Scriptures meant, or who I would be as a man.

I thought again about this man's words. In some ways, I had wrestled with him. I had entered into a man's world, and he had injured me. Perhaps it was just like what Jacob had received from God. Could his words that struck so deeply have actually been a blessing?

———

At the time I was reading Gordon Dalbey's book *Healing the Masculine Soul*. In it he talks about the need for boys to have men in their lives, working, teaching, and showing them life. He went on to quote another man, Robert Bly, who said, "When a father and son do spend long hours together . . . we could say that a substance almost like food passes from the older body to the younger."[2] Gordon wrote that when a boy has a father and other godly men guiding and calling him into manhood, he gets something like a "brown ooze" that covers him and makes him a man.

It was an interesting thought. Dalbey explained in his book, "masculinity bestows masculinity." I thought back to that *American Chopper* show, and wondered if that is what was happening. A father was teaching his sons, letting them fight with him and forge their own thoughts, opinions, and lifestyles—and in the process they were each becoming the men who could handle their work and their world.

As a boy, I was not around many men. I did not grow up in a community where I went on trips with men and hung out over weekends. Men were primarily working at jobs. I realized just recently that because of it, I had grown very suspicious of men over the years. Men were not around me much. Men were in other places, working construction or in business suits, worried about paying the mortgage and their kids' college tuitions, providing for their families, and doing things for us, but never with us. As important as those things may have been, they always seemed irrelevant to my life.

Another author I read named Henri Nouwen once said, "We are facing a generation which has parents but no fathers, a generation in which everyone who claims authority—because he is older, more mature, more intelligent, or more powerful—is suspect from the very beginning."[3] I think he is right. I think it's because we have this deep need for men and fathers, but we have never seen that need met and so don't know what to do with that desire in us. We don't trust men, because so many men have let so many of us down time and again—they haven't been there for us, have hurt us or abandoned us, and yet that desire remains. I could see it in the fraternity. We took our desire for men and fathers to other guys our age who knew no more about them than we did.

During high school and college, I was blind to this. I couldn't see I had a need for real men to show me the way. I can't help but look back now and see how many times I was trying to grow this boy into a man through the approval of guys around me. But they couldn't give me what I needed, they were only boys themselves, and if I was going to find it, I would have to do the things I was most scared of doing to find real men.

One of the first places God wanted me to look for an example was in my relationship with my father. Since I have been living in Colorado and recognizing and dealing with this boy inside, I am coming into a better and better understanding of what the relationship between a father and a son is meant to be.

Over Christmas, my wife and I flew back to Nashville to my parents' house, and my dad gave me a book of our family heritage. As I looked through it, I saw a line of men — fathers and sons. As I looked at it, I realized the distance between my father and I, a lot of which came in many arguments we had growing up. Although we live hundreds of miles away from each other now, I am beginning to feel the need to reconnect and talk through many of those experiences.

Something similar happened to my friend Ben.

After I moved to Colorado, my friend Ben decided to drive from Knoxville to live here for the summer. The plan was for him to get out here, find a job, and enjoy mountain biking, hiking, and fly-fishing with me and some other friends. He wanted to feed his soul with beauty and feed his passion for writing and playing music as he paid his bills. This was a huge trip for him, stepping out on his own, leaving his friends, girlfriend, and family behind to come out here for a few months.

The first few weeks were great for Ben, but the more time he spent out here, and the more time he spent alone, the more something bothered him. As we sat down and talked through it, it all came out. He felt a void inside, a hunger for something deep and masculine. He told me a story about one night when he was in school at Knoxville and he had a fight with his girlfriend. His dad called and left him a message, telling him he was proud of him. Ben laughed and said, "I listened to it twelve or thirteen times that night. I kept playing it over and over."

The more we talked, the more he put words to his need. It was for his father. Ben came to Colorado to step out and into himself, take an adventure, and be more of who he was as a man, but what he felt was the void of not being close to his dad. Ben has an incredible family and a good father, but his dad has worked long hours because of the demands of his business, and with such a huge family, they had not spent a lot of time together as father and son.

Ben decided to do something about it.

So Ben called and shared with his father that he needed him, and told him the story of that phone call, and how he wanted to be around him at work. Ben's father just happens to be a music producer, and yet Ben had never sat and watched his dad in the studio. Ben told him, "I just want to sit and be with you as you do your work. I want to watch and learn and be a part of it." Within three days, Ben had his bags packed, and went back home to spend the rest of the summer with his father.

Just the other day, I realized how far I had come in understanding this in my head, but how little I was actually doing to fulfill this need in my own life now. I knew all about it, I even helped my friend, but I hadn't gone out and done anything about my need in Colorado. I had to ask why. Why, if I knew I needed it, was it not happening in my life? Why are men not teaching, guiding, and fathering me?

As I looked over the past few years of my life living in Knoxville and Colorado, I began to realize God had given me many opportunities to open up with men, and share my needs, but I just hadn't. I had been too scared. I felt too uncomfortable to share my need to be discipled, taught, fathered, and to reveal this young part of me. I either turned men down, drove them away, or ran away when things got a little tough, as I had with my counselor friend. Although I would sit with them over a Bible study, I was too fearful of what they would see when they got to know me or started asking personal questions. I was afraid of being honest and opening up and letting other men see into my heart.

Since living in Colorado, I have met many times with the man who called me a boy. But I just realized the other day, I have never invited him back into that part of me. I have never spoken to him about the boy inside of me. After that day he had called it out, I had protected it. He has become an important guide in parts of my life, and helped me in my writing, and counseled me through other areas, but even after all the time hanging out and all his ability to help me, I have yet to really open up with him and share my real needs and desires with him — the raw, real me. It's crazy, because here is this man who has wisdom, insight, training, and ability, who most guys would jump at the opportunity just to meet with and hang out, but I have been too scared to lay my heart before him.

It is such a vulnerable place, and I am so afraid of being hurt.

I was talking with my friend Matthew and mentioned this to him. He started laughing, and said, "I understand. I have a neighbor, an older man who has been praying with me and offering words of encouragement every so often when I need them. I admire him so much and want to spend more time with him, but I was so afraid to ask him to mentor me." But he risked it, and he did ask. He looked at me embarrassed and said, "Xan, it was easier to ask my wife to marry me than it was to ask this man to mentor me."

I laughed and understood his dilemma.

He went on, "I mean, I knew Christie would marry me, but

I wasn't sure what this man would say. I was so afraid of him saying no, or rejecting me. It was almost too risky to even ask. I couldn't imagine being rejected by this man."

It turned out the man was honored and said, "I would love to." They have recently started meeting together every Saturday morning.

━━

I am more convinced than ever, if we are to find masculinity and step into who we are as men of God, we are going to have to go out and ask for it from someone who has it, and wrestle it from them. I don't think it was meant to be that way. I imagine it is actually the older men who are supposed to do the asking and initiate all of this. But we live in a time and a culture now where that doesn't happen anymore.

I am not joking when I say that asking for others to mentor, teach, guide, and father us is probably the hardest thing to do. Another friend Cory told me the other day, "I find it so hard to step out and ask, yet I can't expect men to just show up at my doorstep and ask to teach me. I am going to have to go out and find it. It's just that it's so hard to do."

As I write this, I am meeting with my counselor friend tomorrow. I called him up yesterday and told him I wanted to talk to him about a few things. I don't want to talk to him about ministry things or writing, but about that boy he called out inside me — the boy in me that, for the first time in my life, I am admitting needs to be fathered. The boy who needs to wrestle, and the boy who needs to be led under men of God. If that boy is to grow up inside of me, then I need to allow Jesus to come for that young place in me, and part of that is asking a man to help me.

I am nervous about it, even as I write this. By tomorrow, I will probably be shaking. I am scared because I have never let anyone into that place in my heart. I have hated and resented the fact that the boy is there and is so needy. I don't like feeling helpless. I am praying that God will bring me the courage to share the real me with this man. I am also scared because I don't know what he will say. He is a busy man, and quite honestly, he might not have the time. I am realizing that it's my job to ask and risk it, and his responsibility to respond. Truth is, whether he does it or not, I need to ask. And I need to find men to help me. I need to trust that God will meet my needs in his time. I need to feel powerless and weak and needy and let the boy out. I have to risk putting my true self on the table, and see if a man will wrestle.

the wildlands

After the suffering of his soul,
he will see the light of life and be satisfied.

The hurricane-like winds were bearing down on us, but despite the wind and elevation, we continued our ascent, cutting through the tall grasses, slowly advancing upward through open hills. We were determined. Our mission was to reach the summit, and the old, rugged cross still miles ahead, rising above the spectacular landscape on the Big Island of Hawaii.

Even at this lower elevation, our view stretched for miles. My heart felt alive surrounded by so many rich colors of deep blues and lush greens. My soul felt at rest with the tall grasses spread out below us like a carpet to the sea, blowing like waves to the edge of the white sandy coast. I felt for a moment as if I were taken back to that boy running through the wildlands—alive and free.

My friend Eric and I came here to take in the beauty and discover this wonder of paradise and the adventures we might have. We had come for ten days to take in all the Big Island had for us. We paddled kayaks to private beaches, snorkeled with manta rays and sea turtles, took out a Zodiac to search for whales, hiked to black sand beaches, and body surfed with our friend Sam who lived on the Big Island and was the real reason we had come.

Our trip was a free gift from him.

We spent our final day hiking up this mountain together.

It is hard to put words to, but we felt desire there. And it was not some photograph or a painting—we were *in it*. I remember thinking, *It doesn't get any better than this.*

And then they appeared.

What began as brown and white specks off in the distance cresting a ridge became a herd of wild horses arriving as if on perfect cue out of some old Western movie. Around twenty-four horses in a pack came at us full speed, then stopped to surround us. The horses stood staring at us, eyes looking wide and curious, nostrils flaring from the exertion of climbing the hilly terrain.

As I looked closer, I saw something in them, strong, un-bridled, wild, and free. They flexed, their muscles twitching; they were patient and intimidating. I saw grace and beauty mixed with a raw strength. The moment was overwhelming, staring at these creatures of such glorious stature. I imagined it was similar to when Adam first saw creation and all the animals in the garden. It was something wonderful, and haunting, almost surreal—more than what my heart could take in.

And then in an instant, they were gone. They left us as fast as they came, running into other open fields. We turned back on our mission, and climbed the rest of the way in relative silence. As we pushed to the top, with my legs burning, we started catching glimpses of the old, wooden cross that rested right at the peak of the mountain, waiting for us.

As we crested the top, I looked at this old, rugged piece of wood, set in the midst of so much beauty and wildness. I placed my hands on it to feel its weathered grain and the grooves the wind and rain had carved over the decades. I held my face up and let the wind cool the sweat on my brow.

It was an odd sensation, but I felt God had written this day especially for me — the massive beauty; the magnitude of the panorama; free, untamed horses that could have trampled me in an instant. I felt as if God wanted me to enjoy it, as if he had sent those horses, and put that cross there for me. He wanted me to take in all this, and remember.

I thought back to many of my questions, and my longings, and what first took me on this quest, and how I had seen the Christian life as a cage, and Jesus as a wheel to run my adventures on. I was wrong. My search took me out of the cage, and into this adventure, and with these friends, and to be surrounded in this beauty, and what I found was the last thing I would have ever expected — God.

As I breathed in and knelt down at the foot of that cross, I closed my eyes and said a small prayer. A prayer of gratitude and hope. Despite all the beauty and wildness around me, it was the cross that held the deepest meaning, and the simplest beauty.

A King had come for me and died for me. A Man had come to bring me into true life — a life of passion, adventure, beauty, strength, and truth. A Man came to restore in me the life I was meant to live. A life filled with God. And not just someday in heaven, but here and now.

It was not an easy trek up the mountain, nor were the past few years of my life. It was hard. I had fallen, struggled, resisted. But as I lifted my eyes at the top of the mountain, I knew it had all been worth it. I was a changed man because of the cross. A man who was growing now, and exploring deep and true things of God and his creation, seeing new wonders, and finding new hope.

It took me years to discover—for God to peel me away and uncover it—but this old, wooden, weather-beaten cross proclaimed the great answer: *Jesus, Jesus, Jesus.* As odd and quirky as it sounded, it was true. And Jesus wasn't just an answer or a wheel. He was a person and alive within me.

As we walked down the mountain and into the daily things of life, something in me knew that Jesus couldn't and wouldn't be confined to a little cage, or a wheel to run adventures on. There was more, more to see, more to find, more to explore and uncover.

Something told me, this is all just the beginning.

notes

Chapter 2: Searching for Life

1. Genesis 3:10.

Chapter 3: Deception

1. *The Matrix*, written and directed by Larry Wachowski and Andy Wachowski, © 1999 Warner Brothers.
2. Ezekiel 28:12-15.
3. Ezekiel 28:17.
4. Revelation 12:7-9,17, MSG.
5. 2 Corinthians 11:14.

Chapter 4: The King

1. Revelation 19:11-16.
2. C.S. Lewis, *Mere Christianity* (San Francisco: Harper San Francisco, 2001), 51.
3. See Micah 5:2. (Herod's scholars quoted this passage to him in Matthew 2:6 when he asked them where the Christ or Messiah would be born.)
4. Zechariah 9:9.
5. Isaiah 53:2.

Chapter 5: The Brotherhood

1. Acts 2:44.
2. Acts 2:46.

Chapter 6: Beauty

1. Psalm 27:4.
2. Psalm 96:6, KJV.
3. 2 Corinthians 4:4.

Chapter 7: The Heart of a Woman

1. Traci Lords, *Underneath It All* (New York: Harper-Collins, 2003), 22-23.
2. Lords, 78.
3. *The Passion of the Christ*, cowritten by Mel Gibson, © 2003 Icon Distribution, Inc. NewMarket Films.

Chapter 8: Strength

1. Genesis 1:26-27.
2. Psalm 62:11-12.
3. From a sermon published on the Internet (Lindale, TX: Community Christian Fellowship, April 18, 2004), http://www.gvccf.org/Sermons/CCF-Service-041804.txt.
4. 1 Timothy 1:18; 6:12.
5. 2 Timothy 2:3.
6. Amos 5:15.
7. Ephesians 6:12.
8. 2 Samuel 22:40.
9. Psalm 18:29, NLT.
10. Psalm 23:3, NLT.

11. Psalm 68:35.

12. Hebrews 11:32-34.

13. Luke 10:27, emphasis added.

Chapter 9: The Role

1. Matthew 9:37.

2. Matthew 23:5-7,27-28.

3. Exodus 3:11,13; 4:1,10,13.

4. Mike Yaconelli, *Messy Spirituality* (Grand Rapids, Mich.: Zondervan, 2002), 14.

5. 1 Corinthians 2:3-5.

6. 2 Corinthians 12:7-9, MSG.

Chapter 10: Wrestling Men

1. See Genesis 32:26-28.

2. Gordon Dalbey, *Father and Son* (Nashville, Tenn.: Thomas Nelson, 1992), 16-17.

3. Henri Nouwen, *The Wounded Healer* (New York: Doubleday, 1990), 30.

about the author

XAN HOOD graduated from the University of Tennessee in Knoxville in 2002. He has worked in both youth and college ministries in Tennessee and is now involved with  the men's ministry in Colorado Springs at the International Anglican Church. He splits his time in Colorado between mountain biking, watching the History Channel, writing, and his new day job as a house painter. He was recently married to Jayne Mincey in 2004 and is founder of The Wildlands, www.thewildlands.com.

For information about speaking events, blog, podcasts, message board, and other resources for this book, visit www.thewildlands.com.